ST JOHN'S WOOD AND MAIDA VALE PAST

Richard Tames

HISTORICAL PUBLICATIONS

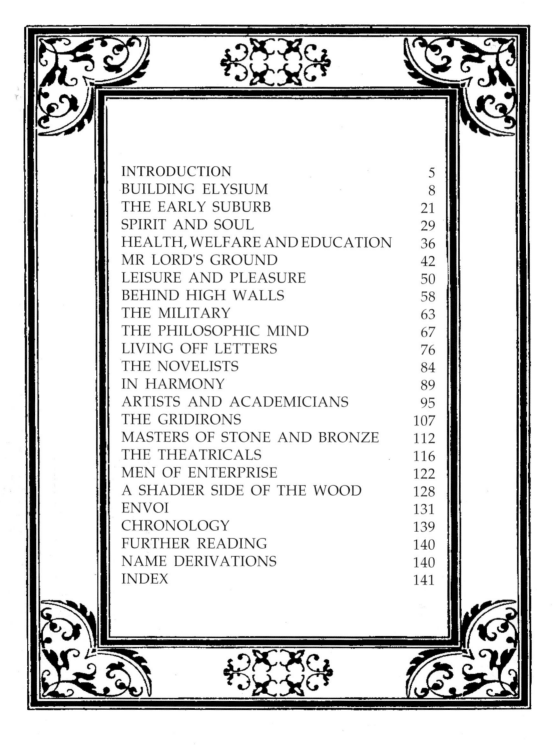

ST JOHN'S WOOD AND MAIDA VALE PAST

First published 1998
by Historical Publications Ltd
32 Ellington Street, London N7 8PL
(Tel: 0171-607 1628)

© **Richard Tames 1998**

ISBN 0 948667 53 2
British Library Cataloguing-in-Publication Data
A Catalogue record for this book is available from the British Library

Typeset in Palatino by Historical Publications
Reproduction by G & J Graphics, London EC2
Printed by Edelvives, Zaragoza, Spain

The Illustrations

Illustrations are reproduced by kind permission of the following:
Roger Cline: *12*
Historical Publications: *6, 7, 9, 11, 14, 15, 16, 17, 18, 20, 23, 26, 27, 30, 31, 32, 33, 36, 39, 41, 43, 45, 47, 48, 49, 52, 54, 58, 59, 63, 64, 65, 69, 70, 71, 72, 76, 77, 81, 82, 83, 85, 86, 89, 90, 91, 92, 93, 94, 96 ,99, 100, 101, 102, 103, 104, 105, 107, 109, 110, 111, 112, 114, 116, 119, 120, 123, 124, 126, 127, 128, 129, 131, 132, 133, 135, 136, 137, 139, 141, 142, 143, 144, 145, 146, 148, 152*
National Portrait Gallery: *147, 153*
Richard Tames: *2, 4, 5, 37, 38, 50, 56, 57, 61, 74, 79, 80, 88, 115, 117, 118, 125, 130, 138, 164*
City of Westminster Archives: *1, 3, 8, 10, 13, 19, 21, 24, 25, 28, 29, 35, 42, 44, 46, 50, 51, 53, 55, 60, 66, 67, 68, 75, 78, 84, 87, 95, 97, 106, 108, 113, 121, 122, 134, 140, 149, 150, 151, 154, 155, 156, 157, 158, 159, 160, 161, 162, 163, 165, 166, 167*

Introduction

"I cannot think why people should think the names of places in the country more poetical than those in London. Shallow romanticists go away in trains and stop in places called Hugmy-in-the-Hole or Bumps-on-the-Puddle. And all the time they could, if they liked, go and live at a place with the dim, divine name of St. John's Wood. I have never been to St. John's Wood. I dare not."

G.K. Chesterton: *The Napoleon of Notting Hill*

Topographically speaking the unique importance of St. John's Wood was underlined by the great architectural historian Sir John Summerson as follows:

"It was the first part of London, and indeed of any other town, to abandon the terrace house for the semi-detached villa – a revolution of striking significance and far-reaching effect."

This book is, however, quite as much about people as place, a matter of biography as much as of topography. Writing in 1913 the historian of St. John's Wood, Alan Montgomery Eyre, summarised the locality tersely as "the district *par excellence* for interesting people". It is difficult to improve on this. Unlike a number of equally affluent parts of London St. John's Wood has long teemed with celebrities. One of the challenges involved in writing this book has been to prevent it from degenerating into a mere social directory or a pastiche of a novel with a Tolstoyan cast list. Even so, the interconnections between the artists, actors, writers and musicians who have inhabited the area at times threaten to become positively Proustian in their complexity.

Some faint idea of the biographical richness of the area can be gleaned by simply listing a few of the personalities which have been omitted. St. John's Wood was, for example, the childhood home of the novelist Wilkie Collins, who was the son of the painter William Collins, of 20 Avenue Road. Press baron Alfred

1. *The quintessential St John's Wood - detached villas in Loudoun Road*

2. The better-known part of Maida Vale – the canal at Blomfield Road.

Harmsworth likewise was raised in Boundary Road in the 1870s and 1880s. Hairdresser Vidal Sassoon grew up in a Jewish orphanage in Maida Vale. Maida Vale was also the chosen refuge of Sigmund Freud, who lived in a hotel there, while a house was being built for him in Hampstead. Samuel Palmer, the biscuit king, chose St. John's Wood for his retirement.

Again, unlike most London suburbs, St. John's Wood has, as a residential area, always had a distinctly cosmopolitan air. One writer described it as "the cynosure of Frenchmen", a description amply borne out by the fact that in the following pages the reader will encounter the great chef Alexis Soyer, the Emperor Napoleon III, the actor Fechter, art-dealer Gambart, painter Tissot and the tight-rope walker Blondin. A similar list could be made

of, say, Germans or Americans, the latter ranging from Constable's biographer, Charles Leslie, to the film actress Lee Remick.

Cosmopolitanism has been accompanied by a certain loucheness. Wilkie Collins' mystery *The Woman in White* draws on the erotic associations of the area. In Michael Sadleir's *Fanny by Gaslight* ' the Wood ' is the setting for a very discreet, very up-market brothel. And even Sir John Betjeman was once moved to muse

   " *What puritan arms have stretched within*
these rooms
      To touch what tender breasts,
      As the cab-horse stamped in the road
outside."

Par excellence for interesting people, indeed.

ce Arms in Ordnance Road at the turn of this century.

1.

5. Italianate detailing on houses in Maida Vale.

6. *A barn belonging to St John's Wood Farm, in the location of today's Underground station.*

Building Elysium

THE FIELDS BENEATH

St. John's Wood was once a tract of the 'Great Forest of Middlesex', populated, if that is the right word, by a huge herd of swine which subsisted on fallen acorns and nuts. Its ancient history still echoes faintly in the names of local roads and sometimes in their alignment as well. The Barrow Hill of Barrow Hill Road is referred to in a Saxon charter of AD986; but when a reservoir was dug on its summit in the early nineteenth century it revealed no evidence of a burial. More likely, therefore, that the name derives from the Old English word *baeruwe*, meaning a grove of wood. Violet Hill was once a medieval lane leading from Lisson village to Kilburn Priory. It lost its former importance when Abbey Road was cut through in the 1820s, but it still marks part of the boundary line between the Harrow School and Eyre estates.

Kilburn Priory, which may have begun as a hermitage on the east side of the high road to Kilburn, was a nunnery and a small and poor one at that.

Boundary Road, which follows the original division between the parishes of Marylebone and Hampstead, now demarcates the City of Westminster from the London Borough of Camden. Grove End Road, now a continuation of Lisson Grove, is shown on early maps as St John's Wood Lane, a winding country cart-track leading to the farm that stood for centuries where the Underground station now is. Langford Place (named in 1867) and Langford Close (named in 1937) commemorate William Langford, who held the manor of Lilestone around 1330.

ROYAL AND ANCIENT

'Great Saint John's Wood', so called to distinguish it from Little St John's Wood near Highbury, takes its name from its medieval owners, the knights of the Order of the Hospital of St John of Jerusalem, known often as the Knights Hospitallers, a fraternity of military monks who followed the rule of St Augustine. The Hospitallers established their first English house at Clerkenwell, then on the northern edge of London, around 1144. St John's Wood, part of the Manor of Lilestone (whence the name Lisson Grove), was by the thirteenth century the property of the other great military brotherhood, the Knights Templars and came into the possession of the Hospitallers in 1323, following the suppression of the Templars. In 1539 the property was confiscated from them by the Crown,

7. *The remains of Kilburn Priory as it appeared in 1722.*

8. *Boundary marks in Boundary Road between the parishes of St Marylebone and St John, Hampstead. Photograph taken in 1951, on the south side, near Finchley Road.*

9. *'The Old Stile in the Boundary Road'.*

as a consequence of the dissolution of religious orders during the Reformation of the English church. The area was subsequently restored to the Order, which was revived under Mary I, but the lands were taken back for the Crown by Elizabeth I. 'Marybone Park' (the northern part of which is now Regent's Park), an area of 554 acres, was enjoyed for royal hunting and girded with ring mound and palings to prevent game escaping. Accounts surviving from 1567-68 record payments for the repair of fencing and a bridge, using timber cut in St John's Wood. It seems probable that, a generation earlier, much timber had been taken from St John's Wood for the building of Hampton Court Palace.

In 1616 one Robert Stacy was being paid the not inconsiderable sum of £20 yearly "for keeping the King's deer in St John's Wood". The wood to the north of the hunting park was actively managed by regular coppicing but it remained sufficiently dense to constitute both a refuge for miscreants and a hazard for travellers. In 1586 Roman Catholic conspirator Anthony Babington hid in St John's Wood after the failure of his plot to assassinate Elizabeth and liberate Mary Queen of Scots. He is supposed to have attempted to disguise himself by hacking off his hair and staining his face with walnut juice but he was eventually driven from cover by hunger and arrested at Harrow after ten days on the run. He subsequently suffered the terrible death assigned for traitors. A more cheerful association exists between the wood and the farcical plot of Ben Jonson's last play, *A Tale of a Tub*, first performed in 1633, which turns on a supposed robbery in St John's Wood.

Following the abolition of the monarchy in 1649 and the consequent confiscation of royal property, St John's Wood was sold in 1650 to William Clarke, a lawyer of the Inner Temple, for £3,645 1s. 8d. At the Restoration it reverted to the Crown once more and in 1668 was granted by Charles II to Henry Bennett, Lord Arlington, who had supported the king in his exile and loaned him much

10. Boundary Road. Woodcut by Ann Gilmore Carter. Date unknown.

11. *The Domesday Survey entry for Lileston Manor, which included St John's Wood.*

money. To pay off these debts Arlington was given an indefinite lease on St John's Wood in return for an annual payment of £13 9s. Needing cash more than land he then sold this on to the Countess of Chesterfield for £7,050. From her line the land was to pass by purchase to the Eyre family in 1732.

FOUR ESTATES

The area dealt with in this book largely consists of four major estates, which, before their development for residential purposes, belonged respectively to the Eyre family, Harrow School, the Dukes of Portland and the Bishopric of London. Until the closing years of the eighteenth century they were regarded as purely agricultural holdings, but thereafter their owners became caught up in the general process of metropolitan expansion which was to transform St John's Wood and Maida Vale into highly desirable residential suburbs.

THE EYRE ESTATE

The eventual exploitation of the Eyre estate was the outcome of a sequence of inactivity, uncertainty and opportunism. In 1732 wine-dealer Henry Samuel Eyre (1675-1754) bought just under five hundred acres of St John's Wood from Philip Dormer Stanhope, 4th Earl of Chesterfield (1694-1773). Eyre had built his fortune out of the politically correct alcoholic preferences of patriotic gentry. In 1703 Britain and Portugal had signed the Methuen Treaty, by which Portugal gave trade preference to English woollens and Britain reciprocated by giving Portuguese wines, notably port and madeira, preference over other wines. This not only proved mutually beneficial but also conferred the additional benefit of spiting France, hitherto Britain's major supplier of wines but by then its mortal enemy in the global struggle for empire.

Lord Chesterfield, a diplomat and aesthete renowned for the smoothness of his manners, was

later to win minor literary fame for initially encouraging Dr Samuel Johnson in his great dictionary project and then ignoring him, thereby provoking a series of celebrated insults. Johnson professed his disappointment at finding that Chesterfield, far from being a Lord among wits, as he had been told, was merely a wit among Lords. When Chesterfield's *Letters to his Son* – a guide to gentlemanly comportment – reappeared in volume form Johnson returned with relish to the attack, denouncing them for teaching "the manners of a dancing-master and the morals of a whore".

In 1732 Chesterfield, who cared nothing for "the rustic, illiberal sports of guns, dogs and horses", was trying to complete the building of a magnificent mansion in newly exclusive Mayfair. It was to finance this project that he parted with his St John's Wood acreage.

The Eyre estate as surveyed in 1733 was no longer the dense forest of Tudor times, most of the greatest trees having long since been felled for metropolitan building needs. It now consisted largely of wooded meadow or pasture, divided into 45 fields, which ranged in size from a cottage garden to more than twenty acres. Here sheep and cattle were fattened for sale or slaughter at Smithfield and hay was harvested to help feed the capital's hundreds of thousands of horses.

There were two major components to the holding. St John's Wood Farm had stood since medieval times on the site of today's St John's Wood Underground station. Cows would still be seen there until the beginning of the twentieth century. The other main farm, centred around a building known as Punker's Barn, or the Red Barn, and a large adjacent cattle pond, was located roughly about a third of the way along St John's Wood Road coming from the Edgware Road end. The home of Sir Edwin Landseer would later occupy its site.

THE EYRE SUCCESSION

Treated as an agricultural property the Eyre lands yielded only a modest return in terms of farm rentals, some £890 per year. Eyre himself was, however, so very wealthy that he could perhaps regard this with indifference, having bought the land more as a status symbol than as a business proposition. When he died in 1754 his estate was valued at £63,651 – at a time when the economic qualification for becoming a Justice of the Peace and therefore being judged of gentlemanly standing – was £100 a year. St John's Wood represented just over a third of Eyre's fortune, being valued at £22,250, a sum equal to 25 years' rentals. This

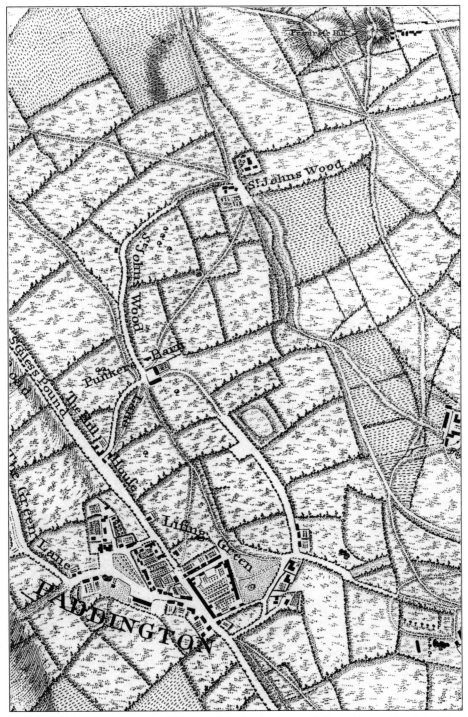

12. *The St John's Wood area in 1746, from John Rocque's map of the environs of London. The lane running N-S to the west of St John's Wood Farm approximates well to today's Wellington Road. Most of the area is shown as rough pasture with very limited signs of cultivation.*

calculation ignored the fact that most of the rents were some thirty months in arrears. This may possibly represent a concession granted in acknowledgment of an outbreak of cattle disease which had struck the Home Counties in 1745 and persisted for an entire decade.

Henry Samuel Eyre died childless and his main beneficiary was his nephew, Walpole Eyre (1735-1773), a godson of the Sir Robert Walpole (1675-1745) who had dominated English politics for a quarter of a century. Walpole Eyre died, along with a dozen others, the victim of a quite spectacular food-poisoning incident, before reaching forty. Although his widow retained a financial interest in the St John's Wood lands until her death in 1823, their effective exploitation would depend on the efforts of the next collateral descendant, Colonel Henry Samuel Eyre of the Guards (there was a Henry Samuel in every generation of Eyres). He died, unmarried, in 1851, passing the property to his nephew, George John Eyre, who died in 1883, his heir being his cousin, the Revd Henry Samuel Eyre and upon his death, in 1890, the property was divided among his five children. The Eyre estate was subsequently leased by the Norwich Union insurance company, which explains why the developments they made in the 1960s bear such Norwich and Norfolk names as Mancroft, Sheringham, Wymondham and Walsingham.

GREAT PLANS AND SMALL BEGINNINGS

A survey of the Eyre estate was made in 1794 by auctioneers Spurrier & Phipps and plans were drawn up to build a sort of miniature Bath with a crescent, a square, a market and a church. But the escalating war against France diverted money and men, including Col. Eyre, from the metropolis. Building fell to a low ebb, as it had done in war-time throughout the eighteenth century, usually reviving when hostilities ceased, as discharged servicemen looked for work and lower taxes left cash to seek profits in property projects.

The Treaty of Amiens in 1802 brought about what proved to be only a brief cessation in the Anglo-French wars; but the interlude was evidently sufficient to revive ambitious ideas for developing St John's Wood. In 1803 and 1804 the young architect John Shaw exhibited at the Royal Academy "An elevated view of the British Circus, proposed to be built by subscription between the Paddington-road and Hampstead on the freehold estate of H.S. Eyre Esq." Shaw's plan envisaged

13. Circus Road c.1906, a vestige of the grand plan for two prestigious crescents.

14. *Alpha Cottages in 1817.   These houses, east of Lisson Grove and south of the Regent's Canal, were demolished when the Great Central Railway extension to Marylebone was constructed.*

an inner and an outer circle of houses, one mile in circumference all told, with 36 dwellings ranged along the inner circle and 66 along the outer one. In the centre there would be a 42-acre 'pleasure ground' for the recreation of the residents. The resumption of hostilities confined this scheme to the drawing-board, though it was not formally abandoned for another five years and there was even talk of reviving it in 1823, when the estate finally passed completely into Col. Eyre's hands. The ghost of what might have been is in the name and alignment of Circus Road, which was to have been the main route of access.

What did survive of Shaw's original conception was, however, a genuine innovation which was to prove a legacy far more enduring than a Bath-style layout – the idea of erecting, not rows or terraces, but houses, singly or in semi-detached pairs, standing in their own gardens.

In 1806 the hack writer Cyrus Redding, who was, decades later, himself a local resident, challenged a correspondent with a beguiling depiction of sylvan bliss:

"Beautiful fields – green lanes, clear air – the very place for lovers of quiet and lovers of Nature – why don't you build a villa in the heart of St John's Wood?".

Redding's vision finally became a reality in the appropriately named Alpha Road, where the first villa was built in 1809. Sir John Summerson, doyen of architectural historians, identified the moving spirit as the architect and designer Charles Heathcote Tatham (1772-1842) who was a protégé of Henry Holland, the son-in-law of 'Capability' Brown and who was himself the architect of the Brighton Pavilion. Holland paid for Tatham to spend two years in Rome, gaining a thorough grounding in classical forms. Tatham's subsequent influence went beyond his own practical work as an architect thanks to his publication of etchings of Roman architecture and neo-classical furniture designs. He also had many artist friends whom he entertained at his new Alpha Road home, including Benjamin Haydon, William Blake and Samuel Palmer. Tatham referred to his residence as a 'cottage' but, if it was, it was a rather grand and self-consciously tasteful one. Summerson regarded it as a crucial model in setting the tone for the subsequent development of the entire locality.

Alpha Road's next significant resident was the Earl of Kingston. This might have been thought to have conferred a certain social cachet on the new neighbourhood; but according to Summerson his lordship was primarily seeking anonymity, being "a sodomite and a drunkard, doomed to insanity". Warming to his theme, Sir John concluded from this choice of address that "almost from the first St John's Wood attracted the odd man out who had sufficient means to be odd without discomfort. While close to London, it was at the back of beyond ..."

THE REGENT INTERVENES

In 1811 the lease on Marylebone Park reverted to the Crown and in the same year the Prince of Wales assumed the title of Prince Regent, his father, George III, having been pronounced insane beyond hope of recovery. The Prince, whatever his many other failings, was a connoisseur of genuine taste and no mean ambition, who desired that his capital should rival Napoleon's in splendour. He therefore commissioned his pet architect John Nash

(1752-1835) to devise a grandiose scheme for a *via triumphalis* linking a projected new summer palace, to be built on Primrose Hill, with Buckingham House, which would be upgraded to displace St James's as the main royal residence. The project was only realised in part – Park Crescent and Regent Street being its major components. The palace on Primrose Hill never got built, nor the dozens of mansions in Marylebone Park which were supposed to finance the rest of the project. But the lodges and terraces which were constructed around the perimeter of what was henceforth Regent's Park gave promise that London was resuming its northwards march.

The construction of the Regent's Canal between 1811 and 1820 initially induced a note of uncertainty but, once its route was settled, it became clear that it would provide an attractive setting for the residences which would be built along what became North Bank and South Bank. Park

15. A map of the Eyre estate drawn up soon after the construction of the Chapel and the relocation of Lord's cricket ground.

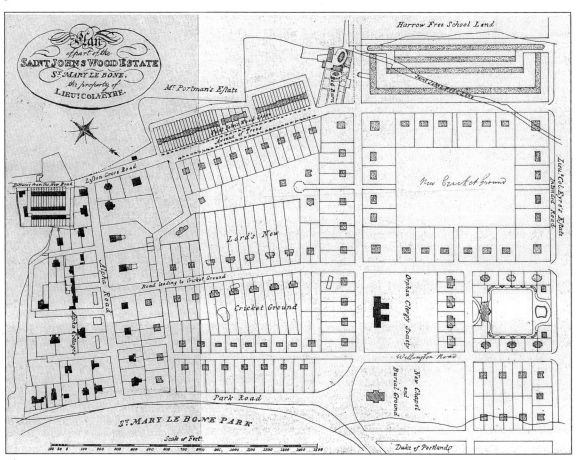

Road, despite being subsequently described rather discouragingly as "a carriage road for the conveyance of corpses to the new Burial Ground", also helped to improve access to the area.

A VISTA OF VILLAS

Even before the ending of the French wars in 1815 the pace of development around the north-west corner of the Park had begun to quicken with the establishment of the Clergy Orphan School in 1812, the building of St John's Wood chapel in 1813 and the opening of Lord's cricket ground at its final and permanent location in 1814. Soon afterwards came the opening of the Eyre Arms Tavern in 1820 and the construction of the Army Riding School in 1825. Building began in real earnest with the opening up of Abbey Road in 1824, Wellington Road in 1826 and 'Finchley New Road' in 1827. The latter, according to the Act of Parliament which authorised its construction, met a long-felt need – "The want of an outlet from the North West side of London to the Great North Road is striking – there being no way to that road west of Tottenham Court Road, although a great proportion of the Noblemen and Gentlemen connected with the Northern districts live in the West". The new route would reach Barnet via Finchley, thereby avoiding the hills of Hampstead and Highgate, a significant consideration in the days of horse-drawn traffic.

The builders who undertook the actual work of construction, on plots leased to them for the purpose, were speculators. It was a risky business. William Hall, after whom Hall Road is named, was a few years too far ahead of demand and is said to have died a pauper in Marylebone poorhouse. The best known builder was James Burton (1761-1837), who had built most of the eastern half of Bloomsbury on the estate of the Foundling Hospital and was Nash's favourite contractor. Burton's far more famous son, Decimus (1800-1881), designer of the celebrated conservatories at Kew Gardens, may well have been responsible for four bow-windowed houses in St John's Wood Road, facing Hamilton Terrace. Decimus was certainly responsible for the design of several major properties nearby, including terraces facing onto Regent's Park and several of its major residences, including The Holme (James Burton's own house) and Hanover Lodge. The other major builders, Chapple and May & Morritt, are less well known but proved capable of turning out pleasing and often original designs, playing on variations of both neo-Classical and neo-Gothic motifs.

To encourage construction of an appropriate standard the Eyre estate made it clear what was

16. *Plan for a turnpike road from Marylebone to Hampstead. This road, the Finchley Road, was approved by Act of Parliament in 1827. It opened up the local estates, particularly the Eyre Estate, to development.*

expected by issuing building leases which specified that properties must be provided with gardens and surrounded by walls at least six feet high. They also forbade the practice of unsocial trades, their definition ranging from laundries to lunatic asylums.

Writing in the early 1830s Thomas Smith, author of *A Topographical and Historical Account of the parish of St. Marylebone* noted with satisfaction that "From St John's Wood Road northwards the prevailing character of the buildings is that of detached villa residences, situated in large gardens, erected in every variety of architectural elegance and occupied by persons of the first respectability". The workaday character of the area had not entirely been erased. The schedules of an insurance policy of 1834 betrays the presence of a laundress called Caldecott occupying a 'tenement and stables' and another tenant named Arundall "who occasionally makes tallow" – not at all the sort of trade one would want conducted at the bottom of one's garden.

It was the construction of broad avenues of detached and semi-detached villas in substantial grounds which was both to give St John's Wood its distinctive character and establish a new model of suburban style, strikingly different from the relentless terraces and sombre squares which had represented the epitome of tasteful planning in the Georgian age.

Thomas Smith had noted that the St John's Wood barracks was "the last pile of buildings at this northern end of the parish". A decade later it was beginning to be surrounded by new streets as the building frenzy reached a peak in the late 1840s, accompanied by a spate of church construction to accommodate the ranks of the respectable. Between 1845 and 1852 thirty-three houses were built in Finchley Road, thirteen in St John's Wood Park, sixteen in Avenue Road and twenty-eight in Boundary Road. Ironically, the very success of the villa mode which made St John's Wood such an eminently desirable residential area also pushed land-prices up so far that later phases of house-building in the 1850s and 1860s witnessed a reversion to terraces and by the 1880s, with the advent of the safety elevator, to the construction of the first apartment blocks.

THE HARROW SCHOOL ESTATE

In 1574 John Lyon, who had founded the Free Grammar School at Harrow in 1571, bequeathed a parcel of land "whereof the profits and yearly rents be employed towards repairing the common highway leading to the City of London" – i.e. the present-day Harrow Road. The area in question, some 42 acres of pasture, rye and gravel pits, bordered what is now Maida Vale. Lyon is remembered in the name of Lyon's Place.

The projected, if initially abortive, schemes for development of the Eyre estate from 1794 onwards, awakened the governors of Harrow School to the potential of their own holdings on the fringe of what promised to become a fashionable residential district. In 1819 Parliament provided the approval necessary to remove a number of legal restrictions on the use of the Harrow lands and gave the governors powers to grant building leases. Construction began from 1823 onwards, somewhat haphazardly, in penny packets of small terraces, on fields sloping down to the main road. Streets were named after the governors of the school – the Duke of Abercorn, the Earl of Aberdeen (himself an Old Harrovian and a future Prime Minister), Lord John Northwick, Charles Hamilton and the Revd J.W. Cunningham, Vicar of Harrow.

The boundary between the Harrow and Eyre estates followed a medieval track which once linked Lisson Green with Kilburn Priory, running via Cunningham Place (once Nightingale Lane) through Hamilton Close and on to Alma Square and Nugent Terrace, to Violet Hill, Blenheim

17. Plan of the Harrow School estate in what is now the Maida Vale area, in 1623.

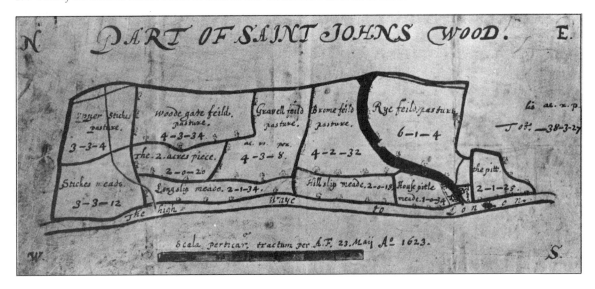

Passage, Greville Road and Priory Road.

Writing in 1885 F. H. Hallam, author o*f Random Sketches of the Parish of Marylebone*, reckoned that the Harrow Estate, which had been worth £100 a year in 1815, had, by 1852, become worth £31,395 annually. Hamilton Terrace was by far the most valuable group of properties, representing over a quarter of the entire total. Others ranked at £2,000 a year or more included Carlton Terrace, Upper Hamilton Terrace, Beaufort Terrace and Northwick Terrace. In the next rank, £1,000-£2,000, came Clifton Road, Marlborough Place, Aberdeen Place and Cunningham Place, with Clarendon Place and Pine-apple Place just below this category.

PORTLAND TOWN

Portland Town, just west of Primrose Hill, proved to be rather a misnomer, at least as far as the Duke of Portland was concerned, for it shared none of the spacious grandeur of Portland Place. When he learned of the poor quality of the buildings being erected there the Duke was alleged to have been furious. But though they doubtless remained an irritant to him and his descendants, their inhabitants proved an invaluable convenience to the residents of the Eyre and Harrow estates, who benefited from their labours as craftsmen and shopkeepers. In 1879 the 5th Duke of Portland died unmarried and the land passed to the de Waldens, to whose descendants it still belongs.

The original Portland Town streets were given rather unimaginative male Christian names - Frederick, Henry, John etc. In 1897, perhaps to mark Victoria's Diamond Jubilee, Charles Street was bastardised to become Charlbert Street, doubtless as a compliment to the Queen's late consort, Prince Albert. If this was meant to raise the tone of the area it did not. Nor did the existence of a substantial sawmill in Lower William Street. Writing in 1905 property surveyor J. G. Head sniffily described Portland Town as being "composed chiefly of small houses, closely packed together, and occupied by a poor class of tenant". The subsequent replacement of these properties by large blocks of apartments was hailed at the time as a major environmental advance. The sawmill disappeared as part of the same upgrading process.

MAIDA VALE

The land on which Maida Vale was built belonged to the Bishopric of London. Building began around 1807, with small blocks, erected by small-scale local builders, appearing along the line of the Edgware Road. By 1828 the stretch of the Edgware

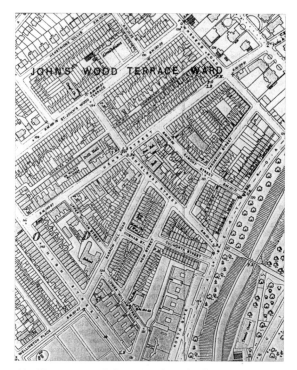

18. *The overcrowded streets of Portland Town in 1913.*

Road beyond Maida Hill was already known as Maida Vale. By 1868 the name was being applied to the whole road between the Regent's Canal and Kilburn and by the 1880s it was used to refer to the entire district which had been developed to the west of it.

The building of Maida Vale was a slower, more hesitant, more drawn out process than the building of St John's Wood. Generally speaking construction proceeded gradually westwards from the line of the Edgware Road and northwards from the Regent's Canal. Warwick Road (now Avenue) had been named by 1840 and Blomfield Road, honouring the energetic and scholarly Charles Blomfield (1786-1857), Bishop of London, by 1841. But in 1857 Bristol Gardens still had open country views to the north and west. James Dolling's map of 1863 showed Clifton Villas being built up but, although Randolph Crescent , Sutherland Crescent and Sutherland Gardens were marked in as streets, no properties were yet indicated as having been built. To the north still lay totally open fields.

Lucas's map of 1887 shows the area between Carlton Road, Kilburn Park Road and Maida Vale as built up. But from Carlton Road southwards to Sutherland Avenue the land was still open, save for the bisecting line of Elgin Avenue, which had an undeveloped Lauderdale Road running off at an angle and a few 'proposed roads' running off at the Shirland Road end. The only clear implication of imminently forthcoming development was the presence of a school on the north side of Elgin Avenue. Much of the area to the north of this was to be saved to become Paddington Recreation Ground (see pp 54-56). As in St John's Wood, around 1900 groups of individual residences in Maida Vale began to be demolished to make way for large mansion blocks of apartments, especially along Maida Vale itself.

WHAT'S IN A NAME?

A number of St John's Wood street names – Acacia, Elm Tree, Grove – refer to the area's sylvan origins. Kingsmill Terrace and Walpole Mews commemorate members of the Eyre family. But others are less straightforward. Gillian Bebbington's *Street Names of London* attributes the naming of Loudoun Road to a desire to mark the memory of the most influential gardening expert of the day, whose name she incorrectly spells as J.C. Loudoun. He was, in fact, J.C. Loudon. The motivation is nevertheless plausible in an emerging garden suburb and the chronology fits because the original Loudoun Villas were built in the 1840s and Loudon died in 1843. The name Loudoun was not, however, applied to the road as a whole until 1871.

There is, however, another feasible explanation for the name, relating to a royal scandal. In 1804 Francis Rawdon Hastings had married Lady Flora Mure Campbell, Countess of Loudoun. Their daughter, Lady Flora Hastings, was appointed a Lady-in-Waiting to the youthful – and as yet unmarried – Queen Victoria. Lady Flora, also unmarried, was afflicted by a liver complaint which led to a swollen abdomen, giving rise to suspicions and rumours of pregnancy, rumours which almost certainly originated from the Queen herself. Medical examination proved Lady Flora to be *virgo intacta*, but the luckless and blameless courtier died of her affliction shortly afterwards in 1839. A year later her heart-broken mother also died and they were buried together at Loudoun Castle. Her father died in 1844, leaving her brother to succeed to two titles, as 2nd Marquis of Hastings and 7th Earl of Loudoun. By then, perhaps, Victoria's personal reputation, having been significantly damaged by her role in the whole wretched affair, had been much redeemed by her joyous marriage to her German cousin, Albert, in 1841. Queen's Terrace and Queen's Grove were so named in memory of the occasion. The memory of the Loudoun *affaire* may, however, have lingered longer elsewhere in the new suburb on account of a local connection, the new Marquis and Earl having had his son baptised in Marylebone parish church in 1832. So, Loudoun Road may enshrine the name of a great gardener – or a royal wrong.

19. Lauderdale Road, one of the principal arteries of Maida Vale's development.

The Early Suburb

THE RESIDENTS

Even by mid-century St John's Wood had acquired a definite tone as a residential district.

Kelly's *Street Directory* designated the more prominent local inhabitants by their titles or professions. The formally titled were, in fact, rather few in number – Lord Nugent, MP for Aylesbury, lived in Langford Place and Sir Frederick Watson in Acacia Road. Some foreign residents, from the world of the arts or diplomacy, styled themselves 'Madame' or 'Signor'. Most residents were styled 'Esquire', but this was still more than an empty courtesy and implied independent means or, at least, a non-manual occupation. The artistic community was represented by several RAs as well as by others who styled themselves 'artist' or 'sculptor'. Any tendency to Bohemianism was offset by the presence of a goodly number of commissioned officers – two colonels and a vice-admiral in Cavendish Road and, on Hamilton Terrace, a major-general, two colonels, two majors, three army captains and a naval captain. Two more major-generals, one a baronet, lived in 'Finchley New Road' and Grove End Road. The professions were represented by surgeons (four on Acacia Road alone) and a couple of engineers but only one accountant. The district's three architects included Alfred Ainger (1797-1859), who had private means and was essentially a dilettante, and Joseph Jopling (1798-1867), who was more a theoretician than a practitioner, specialising in problems of proportion and architectural draughtsmanship. Other residents included a self-styled professor of music, an auctioneer, an 'historical engraver' and an 'omnibus proprietor'.

An article in *Chambers' Journal* in 1849 characterised St John's Wood as 'cosmopolitan' and clearly did not mean this as a compliment, summarising the inhabitants as "men of pleasure, men of substance, men of straw". Conceding the area's attractions for writers and artists who sought seclusion in the interests of their muse, the anonymous author also observed bitchily "in the snugly barred-up cages, with carefully contrived wickets and close gratings, dwell seclusionists of another kind, who pay ready money (rarely are they guilty of such a weakness) to the compilers of Red Books and Court Guides to keep their names *out* instead of putting them *in* and whose servants answer strangers only through the trap".

THE NEWCOMERS

The failure of liberal revolutions across Europe in 1848-1849 led to an English exile for hundreds of frustrated activists and intellectuals. A significant number settled in St John's Wood, where they formed a distinctive coterie.

One central figure was Karl Blind (1826 -1907) who lived at 23 Townshend Road and was almost unique in managing to make a living entirely out of writing, the first recourse for most uprooted word-spinners. Even fellow-refugee Karl Marx grudgingly conceded Blind's industriousness and attributed to him a positive genius for self-advertisement which enabled him to write for British, German, American and Italian magazines and newspapers. The Howitts (see p.78) were helpful in promoting the literary efforts of Blind's less pushy compatriots. Blind was not only good at ingratiating himself with the British – to the disgust of most of his German fellow-exiles – but also at networking with the casualties of other failed revolutions. The Italian Giuseppe Mazzini (1805-1872), a long-term resident of London, was a particular friend and when Blind arranged a meeting with his fervent admirer, Algernon Swinburne, the poet was effusively grateful. Blind also introduced Swinburne to the French revolutionary Louis – 'Property is Theft !' – Blanc (1811-

20. Louis Kossuth, Hungarian patriot and exile.

1882), another St John's Wood resident. In 1866 Blanc, like Ledru-Rollin (1807-1874), yet another French republican resident of the Wood, both wrote letters of condolence to Blind when his stepson, Ferdinand Cohen, committed suicide in a Prussian prison after failing in his attempt to assassinate Bismarck.

Another, far less prolific but even more famous, local personality was Hungarian patriot Lajos (Louis) Kossuth (1802-1894), who lived at 21 Alpha Road. In the eyes of the British populace Kossuth ranked alongside Garibaldi as a hero of national liberation. Unlike Garibaldi, however, he lived out his life in exile and was fated never to see an independent, liberal Hungary.

Sergius Mikhailovich Kravchinski (1852-1895) was a former artillery officer in the Russian army who, after joining the Nihilist movement, stabbed a general and fled into exile, living first of all in Switzerland and Italy, then settling in St John's Wood in 1884. Writing under the romantic pen-name Stepnyak – 'Son of the Steppe' – he wrote a vindication of his terrorist act under the title *Life for Life*, followed by denunciations of Tsarist rule and a novel, translated as *The Career of a Nihilist*. He died, in a fitting aura of mystery, under a north London suburban train.

The most celebrated of all the St John's Wood exiles, the future French Emperor Napoleon III (1808-1873) is dealt with elsewhere (see pp 59-60).

Maida Vale also had its share of exotics. In 1858 the former Queen of the princely state of Oudh, which had been annexed to the British Raj, was living in Warwick Road West and the Rajah of Coorg in Clifton Villas.

SHOPPING

St John's Wood High Street was known at mid-century as High Street, Portland Town. In fact, it had been reduced from a 'high street' once the Finchley Road had been established. Given the absence of facilities for extended food storage in even the wealthiest homes, it was inevitable that any major shopping street would at that time have a large proportion of outlets related to the provision trade, in this instance – one fishmonger, two bakers, two beer-sellers, three cheesemongers, five greengrocers, seven butchers, eight grocers and a 'tripe dresser'. A clear preoccupation with appearance is evident from the presence of six tailors, four boot and shoemakers, three dyers, two milliners, two 'trimming sellers', two hairdressers, a hatter and a retailer of babylinen. There were also two tobacconists but only one chemist. Crafts were represented by makers of blinds and umbrellas and a 'mother of pearl turner'. There were other clusters of shops along Townshend Road and Frederick Street, cowkeepers in Barrow Hill Place, Hill Road, Townshend Road and Charles

21. The hub of local shopping – St John's Wood High Street at the turn of this century.

22. Nugent Terrace c. 1906 – a shopping centre in a back street.

Street and livery stables in Blenheim Terrace, Lodge Place and Grove End Place.

Twenty years later the line-up of food and drink retailers had changed only marginally but fashion was additionally represented by a jeweller, dealers in embroidery and 'Berlin wool' and makers of straw hats and stays. Of the other craftsmen the blind maker was still in business and had been joined by a saddler, an engraver, a cabinet-maker and makers of brushes, trunks and watches and clocks. Changing consumer tastes were reflected in the presence of two coffee rooms, two toyshops and the premises of two 'photographic artists'. The need to refurbish homes which were now no longer new may help to explain the appearance in the High Street of two painter-plumbers, a builder, a carpenter, a gas-fitter and a house decorator.

GARDENS

It was a visit to St John's Wood which moved M. Fiorentino, the musical correspondent of the French newspaper *Constitutionnel*, to observe with evident amazement, "You can hardly believe with what religious care the English cultivate the smallest blade of grass, the most insignificant plant and the commonest flower". According to the painter John Lucas, R.A., "the finest apples and

pears, and by far the finest flowers in England are grown in the nursery grounds of this locality."

The building of St John's Wood coincided with a huge upsurge of interest in gardening. In 1810 there was only one horticultural society in England; by the 1840s there were over two hundred. Much of this can be attributed to the tireless efforts of John Claudius Loudon (1783-1843), publisher of the first popular gardening magazine. The raw streets of the expanding suburb must have housed many eager readers of his *Gardener's Magazine*. Large nurseries, such as those at Pine-Apple Place and Wellington Road, were at hand to supply every need. Large gardens afforded scope for display, experimentation and the construction of

23. Pine-Apple Nursery on the Edgware Road.

24. *Violet Hill, with a few shops. Watercolour: artist and date unknown.*

25. *Gothic fantasy in Langford Place.*

TO THE
Inhabitants of St. John's Wood
AND ITS VICINITY.

W. COOMBER,

Of the Marlborough Tavern, St. John's Wood, and the Proprietor of the Marlborough Omnibuses,

Begs leave to return thanks to the Inhabitants and the Public in general, for the liberal support he has hitherto received, and trusts by strict attention and civility on the part of his Servants, to merit a continuance of the same.

He also takes this opportunity of acquainting them, that the City Atlas Proprietors, the Atlas, Paddington, and Bayswater Associations, have entered into a combination, for the express purpose of Running Off the MARLBOROUGH OMNIBUSES by their united efforts, and at a Meeting convened by them in Paddington, on Wednesday, the 5th. day of October, 1853, it was resolved that Nine City Atlas's, running to the Swiss Cottage should be taken off that road, (to the great inconvenience of the Inhabitants of that district) and sent down to the Marlborough, indirect opposition to his Omnibuses

He, W. C. trusts that the Inhabitants and the Public will please bear in mind, that his were the first Omnibuses that started on that line of Road, direct to and from the City and London Bridge Railways, and also that his Fares are 3d. to and from Tottenham Court Road, and the Great Monopolists, 4d.

greenhouses, many doubtless incorporating Loudon's own invention, the curved glazing-bar which made it possible to design far more elegant constructions than had previously been possible.

Villas with French windows and verandahs virtually invited flowers into the house. Gardening was sufficiently a craze in St John's Wood for Tom Hood to satirize it affectionately by making his flower-loving landlady the heroine of *Mrs. Gardiner, a Horticultural Romance.* Even the impractical George Eliot expressed a pang of regret at her own shortcomings in this particular sphere of practical activity – "The Priory garden might be made much prettier this spring if I had judgment and industry enough to do the right thing".

Flower shows became a perennial feature of St John's Wood life. As early as 1835 a flower fete was held at Lord's in honour of teenage Princess Victoria, the queen-in-waiting. George Eliot's North Bank neighbour, Dr Stewart, "the leading physician of the neighbourhood", sponsored local competitions to encourage the district's humbler inhabitants to submit "plants grown on windowsills, in rooms and awkward places". Flower shows were also a popular method of fund-raising for worthy causes. A gala event at the Pine Apple nursery in 1877 contributed to the costs of the enlargement of the chancel at St Mark's in Hamilton Terrace.

26. *The plaintive voice of Mr Coomber against the plans of larger omnibus companies.*

27. *One of the first cabmen's shelters - in Acacia Road, c.1875.*

HACKNEY CARRIAGES.

DISTANCES

Measured within a Circle of Four Miles Radius from Charing Cross.

ACACIA ROAD, St. John's Wood, STANDING.

TO OR FROM

		MILES	YARDS
pha Road	Alpha Place, St John's Wood		1349
rbour Street East	The Police Court	6	508
aker Street	Marylebone Road	1	248
ank of England	Threadneedle Street	4	829
attersea	St. Mary's Church, Church Road	4	1683
attersea Bridge	Beaufort Street	4	758
attersea Park	Victoria Suspension Bridge	4	144
attersea Park Road	Queen's Road	4	956
attersea Rise	[illegible] Gardens	5	1686
ayswater	Queen's Road [illegible] Gardens	1	1422
edford Square	Bloomsbury	2	871
elgrave Square		2	1518
erkeley Square		2	363
ethnal Green	St. John's Church, Cambridge Road	5	1609
shopsgate Street	Houndsditch	4	1506
lackfriars Bridge	Blackfriars Road	4	223
lackfriars Road	Charlotte Street	4	360
loomsbury Square		2	1522
oltons, The	N.W. Corner, West Brompton	4	3
ond Street	Oxford Street	1	1676
ond Street	Piccadilly	2	869
orough High Street	St. George's Church	4	1340
rixton Hill	Cornwall Road	6	1296
rixton Road	St. Matthew's Church	6	496
runswick Square	St. Pancras		1381
ryanston Square	Marylebone	.	763
uckingham Palace Road	Ebury Bridge		880
uckingham Palace Road	St. James's Park	3	208
adogan Place	Pont Street	3	120
amberwell Gate	The "Red Lion," Walworth Rd.	5	693
amberwell Green	High Street	5	1527
amberwell New Road	Wyndham Road	5	750
amden Road	Brecknock Road	2	946
amden Town	Cobden Statue, High Street	1	1503
amden Town	Mother Red Cap, High Street	1	1132
ampden Hill Road	Upper Phillimore Gardens	2	1681
avendish Square	Marylebone	1	1630
haring Cross	The King Charles Statue	3	143
heapside	Wood Street	4	307
helsea Hospital	Chapel Entrance, Queen's Road	3	1477
hester Square	The Church	3	549
hrist's Hospital	Newgate Street	3	1568
lapham Common	S.E. Corner, Balham Hill Rd.	6	786
lapham Common	The Plough, High Street	5	1426
lapham Park	Clarence Road, King's Road	6	876
larendon Square	Somers Town	2	358
lerkenwell	Rosebery Avenue, Cold Bath Square	3	830
lerkenwell Green	Sessions House	3	1213
ommercial Docks	Plough Bridge	7	818
ommercial Road East	Canal Bridge	6	1287
orn Exchange	Mark Lane	4	1650
ovent Garden Market	Russell Street	3	121
ustom House	Lower Thames Street	4	1489
enmark Hill	Champion Hill	6	765
orset Square	Marylebone	1	132
owning Street	Treasury Passage	3	703
aton Square	The Church	3	4
ccleston Square	Pimlico	3	832
dgware Road	Marylebone Road	1	667
lephant and Castle	Newington	4	1050
uston Road	Judd Street	2	966
uston Road	Tottenham Court Road	1	1679
uston Square	St. Pancras	2	359
insbury Square	City Road	4	1041
itzroy Square	St. Pancras	1	1514
leet Street	Fetter Lane	3	1041
ulham Road	Stamford Bridge	4	1120
loucester Road	Queen's Gate Terrace	3	782
loucester Square	Paddington	1	1372
olden Square	St. James's	2	858
reat Queen Street	Freemasons' Tavern	3	136
reen Lanes	Petherton Road	4	1383
rosvenor Place	Chapel Street	2	1260
rosvenor Square	Mayfair	1	1528
rove End Road	Circus Road, St. John's Wood		546
uildhall	King Street, Cheapside	4	682
ackney	Well Street, Mare Street	6	148
ackney Road	Great Cambridge Street	5	234
amilton Terrace	Abercorn Pl., St. John's Wood		980
ammersmith	North End Road, Edith Road	4	263
anover Square		2	155
arley Street	Devonshire Street, Marylebone	1	1029
erne Hill	The Half Moon	7	106
igh Holborn	Chancery Lane	3	517
igh Holborn	Gray's Inn Road	3	698
igh Holborn	Southampton Street	2	1704
olborn Circus		3	997
OSPITALS:—			
Bethlehem	Lambeth Road	4	690
Charing Cross	Agar Street, Strand	3	226
Consumption	Fulham Road, Brompton	3	1303
German	Ritson Road, Dalston	5	593
Great Northern	Holloway Road	3	957
Guy's	St. Thomas's Street, Borough	4	1569
King's College	Portugal Street	3	457
Lock	Dean Street, Soho	2	829
Lock	Harrow Road	1	491
London	Whitechapel Road	5	1350
London Fever	Liverpool Road, Islington	3	1158
Lying-in	Endell Street, Long Acre	2	1500
Lying-in, General	York Road, Lambeth	3	1681
Lying-in, London	City Road	4	652

		MILES	YARDS
HOSPITALS—continued.			
Lying-in, Queen's	Marylebone Road	1	478
Middlesex	Mortimer Street, Marylebone	2	336
Royal Free	Gray's Inn Road	3	103
St. Bartholomew's	West Smithfield	3	1568
St. George's	Hyde Park Corner	2	1078
St. Luke's	Old Street	4	652
St. Mary's	Cambridge Place, Paddington	1	1021
St. Thomas's	Westminster Bridge	3	1416
University	Gower Street, St. Pancras	2	281
Westminster	Broad Sanctuary	3	1028
Hyde Park Corner	The Lamp Post	2	1037
Islington	The Angel	3	766
Kennington Park Road	Brixton Road	4	1639
Kennington Road	Kennington Lane	4	1438
Kensington	The Church, High Street	2	1610
Kensington Road	(Centre of Kensington Crescent)	3	1213
Kensington Road	Rutland Gate	3	217
Kentish Town Road	Fortess and Highgate Roads	2	785
Kilburn Park Road	Edgware Road		1579
King's Cross		2	1288
King's Road, Chelsea	Man in the Moon	4	573
King's Road, Chelsea	Sydney Street	3	1685
Knightsbridge	Sloane Street	2	1647
Ladbroke Grove	St. John's Church	2	876
Lambeth Bridge	Millbank Street	3	1673
Lambeth Palace		4	310
Leadenhall Street	Lime Street	4	1306
Lincoln's Inn Fields	Serle Street	3	656
Lisson Grove	Marylebone Road	1	336
Lombard Street	Birchin Lane	4	957
London Bridge	Adelaide Place, City	4	1234
London Docks	Upper East Smithfield	5	791
Long Acre	St. Martin's Lane	2	1601
Loughborough Road	Cold Harbour Lane	6	316
Lowndes Square	Knightsbridge	2	1636
Ludgate Circus	City	3	1416
Maida Hill	Aberdeen Place, Edgware Road		1531
Manchester Square	Marylebone	1	1058
Mansion House	City	4	733
Marble Arch	Oxford Street	1	1407
Marlborough Road, Chelsea	Whitehead Grove	3	1097
Marylebone Road	Albany Street	1	1191
Marylebone Road	St. Marylebone Church	1	549
Metropolitan Cattle Market	S.E. Corner	2	1462
Mile End Road	Cambridge Road	5	1672
Mint	Tower Hill	5	434
Montagu Square	Marylebone	1	639
Notting Hill	Pembridge Square	2	460
Notting Hill Square	Uxbridge Road	2	1210
Oakley Street, Chelsea	Cheyne Walk	4	501
Old Bailey	Central Criminal Court	3	1625
Old Broad Street	Winchester Street, City	4	1249
Old Kent Road	Canal Bridge	6	576
Onslow Square	Brompton	3	1158
Oxford Street	Regent Circus	2	289
Oxford Street	Tottenham Court Road	2	1013
Paddington Green	The Church	1	429
Pall Mall	War Office	2	1403
Park Lane	Grosvenor Gate	2	43
Park Lane	Stanhope Gate	2	408
Park Square	Regent's Park	1	817
Parson's Green	Rectory Road	5	667
Peckham	High Street, Rye Lane	6	1540
Penton Place	Amelia Street, Walworth	5	196
Piccadilly	Half Moon Street	2	932
Piccadilly	Regent Circus	2	1231
Pimlico	Army Clothing Depôt, Grosvenor Road	4	80
Portland Place	Weymouth Street	1	1297
Portman Square	Marylebone	1	933
Post Office (General)	St. Martin's-le-Grand	4	144
Queen Anne's Gate	Western Side, Westminster	3	745
RAILWAY STATIONS:—			
Aldersgate Street	Metropolitan	4	136
Barnsbury	North London	3	303
Broad Street	North London	4	1404
Brixton	Chatham and Dover	6	71
Camden Town	North London	1	1582
Cannon Street	South-Eastern	4	798
Charing Cross	South-Eastern	3	315
Clapham Junction	South-Western	5	1491
Clapham Road	Chatham and Dover	5	1665
Dalston Junction	North London	4	1718
Edgware Road	Metropolitan	1	502
Euston	North-Western	2	638
Farringdon Street	Metropolitan	3	1330
Fenchurch Street	Blackwall	4	1605
Gloucester Road	Metropolitan	3	1250
Highbury	North London	3	1273
Kensington	Addison Road	3	1260
King's Cross	Great Northern	2	1138
Liverpool Street	Great Eastern	4	1579
London Bridge	London and Brighton	4	1705
Ludgate Hill	Chatham and Dover	3	1499
Mansion House	Metropolitan District	4	486
Moorgate Street	Metropolitan	4	1019
Notting Hill	Hammersmith and City	2	600
Old Kent Road	South London	6	1662
Paddington	Great Western (Departure)	1	1094
Queen's Road	South London	7	304
St. Pancras	Midland	2	1091

		MILES	YARDS
RAILWAY STATIONS—continued.			
Spa Road	South-Eastern	5	1736
Vauxhall	South-Western	4	526
Viaduct, Holborn	Chatham and Dover	3	1359
Victoria, Centre of Frontage		3	279
Waterloo	South-Western (Main Line)	3	1639
Westbourne Park	Great Western	1	1356
West Brompton	Metropolitan District	4	278
Red Lion Square	Holborn	3	127
Regent's Park	Cumberland Terrace (Centre of)	1	108
Regent's Park	Hanover Gate		1012
Regent Square	St. Pancras	2	1504
Regent Street	Langham Place (The Church)	1	1714
Russell Square	Bloomsbury	2	1022
St. George's Circus, Southwark	The Obelisk	4	520
St. George's Square	Lupus Street, Pimlico	3	1436
St. James's Square	St. James's	2	134
St. James's Street	King Street	2	117
St. John's Wood	The Eyre Arms, Finchley Road		
St. John's Wood Park	Avenue Road		1070
St. Katherine's Docks	Bridge	5	857
St. Pancras Workhouse	King's Rd., Camden Tn.	2	246
St. Paul's Churchyard	Ludgate Hill	3	173
Shaftesbury Avenue	Broad Street, Bloomsbury	2	1313
Shepherd's Bush Green	(East End of)	3	707
Sloane Square	Chelsea	3	764
Smithfield	Meat Market, West Entrance	3	1423
Soho Square		2	927
Somerset House	Strand	3	457
Southampton Street	The Crescent, Camberwell	6	561
Southwark Bridge	Queen Street Place	4	839
Southwick Crescent	St. John's Church	1	1117
Spitalfields	Christ Church, Church Street	5	190
Stepney Green	King John Street	6	1013
Stockwell	The Swan, Clapham Road	5	517
Stoke Newington Road	Wellington Road	5	537
Strand	Law Courts	3	760
Tavistock Square	St. Pancras	2	707
THEATRES, Places of Amusement, &c.:—			
Adelphi Theatre	Strand	3	290
Agricultural Hall	Upper Street, Islington	3	1218
Albert Hall	Kensington Road	2	1720
Alhambra	Leicester Square	2	1627
Astley's Theatre	Westminster Bridge Road	3	1532
Botanic Gardens	Regent's Park	1	802
British Museum	Gt. Russell St., Bloomsbury	2	1449
Court Theatre	Sloane Square	3	779
Covent Garden Theatre	Bow Street	3	16
Criterion Theatre	Piccadilly	2	1256
Drury Lane Theatre	Catherine Street	3	181
Exeter Hall	Strand	3	436
Gaiety Theatre	Strand	3	385
Garrick Theatre	Charing Cross Road	2	1698
Globe Theatre	Newcastle Street, Strand	3	481
Grand Theatre	High Street, Islington	3	884
Haymarket Theatre		2	1523
Lord's Cricket Ground	St. John's Wood Road		946
Lyceum Theatre	Wellington Street, Strand	3	310
Lyric Theatre	Shaftesbury Avenue	2	1307
Madame Tussaud's	Marylebone Road	1	330
Marylebone Theatre	Church St., Marylebone		1729
National Gallery	Trafalgar Square	3	103
Natural History Museum	Cromwell Road	3	703
Olympic Theatre	Wych Street, Strand	3	431
Oval	Kennington (Surrey Cricket Ground)	4	1389
Pavilion Theatre	Whitechapel Road	5	1120
Prince of Wales's Theatre	Coventry St.	2	1382
Princess's Theatre	Oxford Street	2	605
Royal English Opera House	Cambridge Circus	2	1316
Royalty Theatre	Dean Street, Soho	2	1014
Sadler's Wells Theatre	St. John's St. Rd.	3	1125
St. James's Hall	Regent Street	2	107
St. James's Theatre	King Street, St. James's	2	1247
Shaftesbury Theatre	Shaftesbury Avenue	2	131
Standard Theatre	Shoreditch High Street	4	1635
Strand Theatre	Strand	3	57
South Kensington Museum	Cromwell Rd.	3	650
Surrey Theatre	Blackfriars Road	4	56
Vaudeville Theatre	Strand	3	333
Victoria Hall	Waterloo Road	3	1696
Zoological Gardens	[illegible] Regent's Pk.		1724
Torrington Square	Bloomsbury	2	703
Tottenham Court Road	Francis Street	2	375
Tower of London		5	34
Tufnell Park Road	Carlton Road	3	572
Uxbridge Road	Porchester Terrace	1	1743
Uxbridge Road	Victoria Gate, Hyde Park	2	53
Vauxhall Bridge	Vauxhall Bridge Road	4	6
Victoria Park	Approach Road	6	55
Walham Green	The Church	4	1473
Wandsworth Road	Cedars Road	5	562
Wandsworth Road	Priory Road	5	190
Warwick Square	Pimlico	3	1108
Waterloo Bridge	Waterloo Road	3	955
Westbourne Terrace	Bishop's Road	1	86
West London Cemetery	Fulham Rd., Brompton	4	828
Westminster Bridge	Bridge Street	3	1016
Westminster Bridge Road	Kennington Road	4	265
Westminster Ho. of Par.	Centre of Palace Yd.	3	1026
Whitehall	Horse Guards	3	433
Wimpole Street	Great Marylebone Street	1	1269
"York and Albany"	Regent's Park	1	682

28. The location of a major cab rank at Acacia Road meant that distances all over London, even down to the last yard, had to be displayed. Issued by the Metropolitan Police in 1891.

29. *The impressive terraces of Carlton Hill proclaimed the attractions of northern St John's Wood.*

THE SUBURB SURVEYED

W.S. Clark's *The Suburban Homes of London: A Residential Guide*, published in 1881, was gushing in its approbation of an area which had by then been virtually built-up:

> "St John's Wood has a brief history in point of date, but a rich one in associations ... There meet together ... the eminent in every department of London life, and yet there is no place where persons are more isolated. ... The seclusion that distinguished the residences in St John's Wood is favourable to the pursuits of art and literature, and makes it in some respects the very best locality for individuals so engaged."

And, as for those lesser mortals condemned by the contrasting ordinariness of their talents to earn their livelihood by less glamorous means, they could take consolation in reflecting that they could at least make their way to the abodes of commercial servitude in comfort – "the railway and omnibus accommodation is of the best as to quantity and the omnibus especially as to quality. No better-appointed conveyances enter London."

The same author apparently regarded the development of Maida Vale for residential purposes as a transformation little short of the miraculous – "roads, crescents, terraces – on what within modern times was a hopeless desert ... the rudeness of Nature ... and the degraded forms and habits formerly prevalent have been made to give place to culture, piety and comfort ".

30. *St John's Wood Chapel c.1828.*

31. *Thomas Hardwick, the Chapel's architect.*

Spirit and Soul

FROM CHAPEL TO CHURCH

St John's Wood Chapel was built in 1813 on a site donated by the Duke of Portland some twenty years previously and consecrated in 1814. The first minister was the Rev. Thomas Wharton MA, who also doubled as Master of the Clergy Orphan School which stood just across the way. The architect, Thomas Hardwick (1752-1829) had, at the age of seventeen, won the first ever Silver Medal for architecture to be awarded by the Royal Academy and trained under Sir William Chambers, doyen of the profession. Hardwick in turn advised one of his pupils, J.M.W. Turner, to try painting instead of architecture. Despite the opportunities offered by the development of St John's Wood, Hardwick made his career out of designing public buildings, rather than houses, and by taking on responsibility for the maintenance of such historic sites as Hampton Court and Kew Palace.

Strictly speaking, St John's Wood's new house of worship was only a chapel-of-ease, subordinate

initially to the parish church of St Marylebone and from 1899 to Christ Church, Cosway Street. Nevertheless, St John's Wood Chapel was habitually referred to as a Church long before it was formally constituted as such in 1945. It became St John's Wood Parish Church in 1952.

Marylebone parish church on the Marylebone Road was also designed by Hardwick and is thought to be his best work. Both buildings are distinguished by a bold portico and prominent cupola.

James Elmes, writing in 1827, characterised the Chapel condescendingly as "substantial, unpretending ... a very useful and appropriate building but of a fashion that is now gone by". Thomas Smith, writing in 1833, noted that, although the interior had not been painted since its consecration "it appears as fresh and clear as at the first day, which can only be accounted for by the purity of the atmosphere and absence of surrounding buildings". The high social standing of the congregation was attested by the presence of funerary monuments designed by such leading artists as Sir Francis Chantrey, William Behnes and Edward Blore. Smith characterised them as "most beautiful specimens of modern sculpture,

by the most celebrated professors of the age" but also noted with some dismay that "the sum charged for permission to erect a monument in this chapel is so enormous, that it amounts almost to a prohibition". Early burials included the eccentric millionaire John Farquhar (see p.122), Academician John Jackson (see p.95), no less than four East India Company lieutenant generals and the widow of Benjamin West, the American painter who became President of the Royal Academy. West had promised an altar-piece for the new chapel but was himself interred with much ceremony in St Paul's Cathedral before he could redeem his pledge. Another distinguished artist buried in the Chapel churchyard was Irish-Italian Peter Turnerelli (1774-1839). Born in Dublin, he taught members of the royal family as Sculptor-in-Ordinary and twice declined a knighthood. Turnerelli pioneered the depiction of his subjects in contemporary dress, rather than classical costume, thereby bringing to sculpture a mode of treatment which West had introduced in relation to painting historical events.

Writing in 1846 Frank Morrison noted that the St John's Wood Burial Ground was "now so densely crowded as it might be taken for the place of sepulture of a mighty nation rather than the

32. St John's Wood Chapel c.1906.

depository for the dead of a portion of what were recently "out parishes of the Metropolis". Within ten years of its opening the six-acre site was accommodating 1,260 burials a year. By 1830 the figure had risen to 1,743 and by the year in which Morrison was writing to 2,163, of whom 577 were paupers. This would amount to an average of half a dozen funerals every single day of the year. The Burial Ground was laid out as a garden in 1886.

According to A.M. Eyre, opposite the entrance to St John's Wood churchyard, "at the crossroads with a stake in his inside", lies the body of J. Morland, murderer and suicide. Morland had been a servant of Sir Charles Warwick Bampfylde. Following his dismissal, but while his wife yet remained in Bampfylde's service, Morland, convinced (quite wrongly) of an affair between his wife and his former employer, kept watch outside the baronet's house in Montagu Square and, on 7 April 1823, shot him as he came out. He then put a pistol in his own mouth and blew his brains out. Bampfylde lingered for twelve days before dying.

THE GALLINI GIFT

A.M. Eyre attributed the building of the Roman Catholic Church of Our Lady in Grove Road in 1836 to the "munificence of two maiden ladies of the name of Gallini, whose father, an Italian refugee, had settled in London, and having taught dancing to sundry members of the royal family, became Sir John Gallini ... ". The ladies themselves derived a goodly income from their ownership of the fashionable concert-room in Hanover Square. The architect chosen was J.J. Scoles (1798-1863), who specialised in building Catholic churches. In his youth he had travelled adventurously throughout the Middle East and in 1835 he became one of the original founding members of the Institute of British Architects. His masterpiece is the Church of the Immaculate Conception, in Farm Street, Mayfair, headquarters of the Jesuit order in England.

Writing in 1897 Walford in *Old and New London* dismissed Scoles' Grove Road effort as "a rather poor reproduction of some of the features of the Lady Chapel in St Saviour's, Southwark". If that was so, at least Scoles could be accused of bearing sound historical models in mind. Professor Pevsner, writing in the 1950s, makes no criticism of the building, which, by his frequently acerbic standards, almost amounts to a compliment.

33. *St Mark's church, Hamilton Terrace.*

DUCKWORTH'S DOMINION

St Mark's, Hamilton Terrace was built in 1845-46 by Thomas Cundy junior (1790-1867), who was routinely assisted by his third son, also Thomas (1820-1895). Cundy *pere* was surveyor to the Grosvenor estate and built six other churches in London. The consecration, in 1847, was performed by Charles Blomfield (1786-1857), the energetic Bishop of London and eminent Greek scholar, after whom Blomfield Road, Maida Vale is named. Built at a cost of £9,330, St Mark's was intended to seat a congregation of 1,450. Its internal spaciousness was designed to provide the preacher with maximum visibility and audibility but did not recommend it to the architectural historian Goodhart-Rendel who dismissed it as 'a large Gothic riding-school '.

One of the earliest incumbents of St Mark's, the impressively named John Chippendall Montesquieu Bellew, was famed as a great preacher. His son, Harold Kyrle Bellew, evidently inherited some of his talent and became a noted actor. Bellew senior may unwittingly have signalled his future path when he donated four surplices to the new church, for he later converted to the Roman church.

The man who undoubtedly made St Mark's a resounding success was Robinson Duckworth (1836-1911). Duckworth had taken a First in Classics at Oxford, where he had been a friend of Charles Dodgson, the author of *Alice in Wonder-*

34. *Canon Duckworth, Vicar of St Mark's.*

land and, as 'the Duck', had been a member of the immortal Oxford boating-party which had inspired the original story.   Having served as tutor to Prince Leopold, the Duke of Albany, Duckworth was appointed Vicar of St Mark's in 1870, the same year in which he was appointed Chaplain in Ordinary to Queen Victoria. Five years later he became a Canon of Westminster Abbey in succession to the author Charles Kingsley. Duckworth, who lived at 5 Abbey Road and 77 Hamilton Terrace, got Stacy Marks, who lived at No. 17 (now 40), to design his coat of arms. In 1875 Duckworth was also appointed Honorary Chaplain to the Prince of Wales, accompanying him on his 1875-6 tour of India, and in 1891 Duckworth took on further responsibilities as Rural Dean of St Marylebone.

Duckworth was, perhaps predictably in view of his various offices, one of the earliest recipients of the Royal Victorian Order, instituted in 1896 by the Queen to acknowledge personal service to the Royal Family. Under his well-connected leadership expansion and improvement became the order of the day at St Mark's. By 1873 the parish schools on Violet Hill had been completely rebuilt, providing purpose-built places for 700 where for-

merly there had only been an iron shed capable of taking eighty. In 1874 a fine window was donated by the parents of the artist Sigismund Goetze, who was himself later to design the memorial to Charles Erskine. Five panels of the reredos, depicting works of Christian charity, were painted by Edward Armitage RA, whose studio was in Hall Road. (Armitage could afford to dwell on thoughts of charity: he left £318,000 at his death, a fabulous legacy, greater than any other Victorian artist.) In 1878 another window was donated in memory of two little girls who had died of diphtheria. By that time a major programme to expand the chancel was under way, the Duke of Albany, Duckworth's former pupil, laying the first stone in 1877. A wrought-iron screen at the entrance to the chancel commemorates the Duke's connection with St Mark's. In 1882 the front panels of the organ were decorated in memory of Gertrude, the wife of singer Sir Charles Santley (see p.90). The organ, "one of the largest and finest-toned in London", plus the presence in the congregation of eminent professional musicians like Santley, ensured that "the St Mark's Parish Concerts, at which rich and poor were brought together, enjoyed ... a very high reputation". Duckworth was prone to preach against "the influence of the weekend habit and the growth of a restless passion for amusement and wild locomotion" (although he did list his own recreations as 'music and foreign travel'); but he maintained the loyalty and affection of his congregation until his retirement as Vicar in 1906. The baptistry was added to St Mark's in Duckworth's memory.

The First World War witnessed a dramatic decline in both the size of the congregation and the finances of the church, compounded by a liturgical foray in the direction of Rome, which weakened attendance still further. Both were remedied between the wars but St Mark's suffered significant damage during the last war and the spire was not repaired until 1955. During the war Royal Air Force recruits, posted in St John's Wood for kitting out and preliminary assignment, made up a large part of many congregations. 1997 witnessed the celebration of St Mark's sesquicentenary – no mean achievement in an area in which so many of the churches founded in the same era had been entirely swept away.

A CHOICE OF CHURCHES
Space precludes more than a brief mention of just some of the other local places of worship.

All Saints, Finchley Road was built in 1845 on a site donated by Col. H. S. Eyre, who also contributed £1,000 towards the building costs. W.S.

Clark characterised it as "the fashionable and first", although Goodhart-Rendel's aesthetic judgment was characteristically brusque – "general plan rather particularly weak". Consecrated in 1846, All Saints finally closed in 1974 and was demolished in 1978 to make way for the construction of 'The Terraces' .

St Saviour's, Warwick Avenue was built in 1855-56 by Little, the same architect who had designed All Saints. Goodhart-Rendel put it in the same category as St Mark's: " just a riding school", although he exempted the chancel, ambiguously commending it as "very rich and Commercial ". The original St Saviour's was demolished in 1972. Goodhart-Rendel's reaction to its striking successor must be imagined.

Nonconformists had the option of attending Emanuel church, Northwick Terrace (1833-4), the Presbyterian church opened on Carlton Hill in 1851, the Congregational chapel in St John's Wood Terrace, or the Baptist Church of 1863 in Abbey Road, where the future Abbey National Building Society was to be founded in 1874.

St Paul's, Avenue Road was built in 1864-5 by S.S. Teulon. Writing shortly before its demolition in 1958 Professor Pevsner described its east front as displaying all the architect's "sense of sensational display, crude, heavy, noisy and impressive". (The same doyen described the same architect's St Stephen on Rosslyn Hill as having "more dignity than the earlier St Paul, Avenue Road, but with the same unmistakable Teulonesque hamfistedness".)

All Souls, Loudoun Road, opened in 1865, was established by the Revd Henry Robinson Wadmore, who remained its incumbent until 1890, when he became Bishop of London. The architect of the church was Wadmore's own brother, James.

St Stephen's, Avenue Road, was described by W.S. Clark in 1881 as "a lovely church in its sweet retirement under Primrose Hill".

One church which did win Pevsner's approval was the Catholic Apostolic Church begun in Maida Avenue in 1891. It was designed by the very eminent John Loughborough Pearson (1817-1897), architect of Truro cathedral. Pevsner judged this, one of Pearson's last efforts, to be "too little known among his works".

SYNAGOGUES

By the 1880s it was reckoned that between one thousand and two thousand of Maida Vale's estimated ten thousand residents were Jewish. Prominent among these were the industrialist Sir Ludwig Mond and the poet Mathilde Blind. To

35. *The Congregational church in St John's Wood Terrace. It is now, minus the cupola, used as a recording studio.*

36. *(Left) All Saints church in Finchley Road, from The Builder, August 1846.*

37. *(Below) The Baptist church in Abbey Road. The architects were W.G. Habershon and Pite.*

38. *(Above) The Spanish and Portuguese Synagogue at the corner of Ashworth and Lauderdale Roads was designed in a Byzantine style by Davis and Emmanuel, 1896.*

serve the spiritual needs of this sizable community the New London Synagogue was built in Abbey Road in 1882 to designs by H.H. Collins. The synagogue built in St John's Wood Road in 1925 to designs by Messrs Joseph was gnomically characterised by Pevsner as 'Liberal indeed'.

A PROPHETIC POSTSCRIPT

Joanna Southcott (1750-1814), domestic servant, spinster and fervent Methodist, lived unremarkably in her native Devon until she was forty-two, when she suddenly proclaimed herself to be prophetically gifted. Slowly building a small but devoted following, she took her mission to Bristol in 1798 and in 1801 published her first work *The Strange Effects of Faith*. In 1802 she came to London, where, after touring industrial districts of the North of England, she based herself henceforth. Declaring that only 144,000 souls were destined for salvation Joanna commenced "sealing the faithful" by distributing written guarantees of passage to paradise among her adherents.

In 1813 the self-proclaimed prophet, now over sixty, declared in her *Third Book of Wonders* that she would shortly give birth to a second Christ, called Shiloh. Withdrawing into a strict confinement in October, she became ill in March 1814 and died later that year, probably of a brain tumour. The symptoms of her 'pregnancy' are probably to be accounted for by dropsy. She was buried, in an unmarked grave, in the common ground of the newly consecrated churchyard of St John's Wood Chapel, the deceased being referred to throughout as 'Goddard'.

Despite the fact that her funeral was attended by only four mourners, and despite the hollowness of her various prophecies and the somewhat ludicrous circumstances of her death, the memory of Joanna Southcott was sustained by a dedicated band of adherents. Fourteen years after her demise tablets to her memory were erected in the chapel and a further fourteen years after that, in 1842, her imminent resurrection and the birth of Shiloh were still eagerly anticipated. When Joanna Southcott failed to materialise her followers were left looking forward to her final legacy – the opening of a mysterious box in the presence of twenty-four bishops. When it was finally opened, in 1927 (in the presence of one obliging bishop) it was found to contain a few coins, a pistol, a dice-box, a nightcap, a trashy romantic novel – and a lottery ticket.

39 Joanna Southcott.

JOANNA SOUTHCOTT.

40. The memorial to Joanna Southcott in St John's Wood churchyard. A tablet was erected in 1828, but replaced by this stone in 1865.

Health, Welfare and Education

" ... *the air of St. John's Wood is as pure as any in England owing to its high elevation and perfect drainage. I have the authority of an old retired physician, residing in the neighbourhood, for saying that this is the Montpelier of London.*"

Thus wrote the painter John Lucas, RA, a resident of St John's Wood Road, in 1872. In an age in which it was still widely believed that most infectious diseases were contracted through breathing in the foul-smelling 'miasma' that permeated slum areas the healthful advantages of suburban life seemed self-evident. Professional housewife Mrs. J.E. Panton, author of *From Kitchen to Garret* and *Suburban Residences and How to Circumvent Them*, warned her readers that new suburbs were 'not Paradise' but they did have the inestimable asset of fresh air, although she also warned against moving into brand-new houses on the grounds that their drains were untested. The salubrity of suburbs was, in any case, perennially advertised by estate agents just in case any prospective client was foolishly inclined to overlook the benefits they would be conferring on their loved ones by moving to a leafy avenue of well-spaced villas remote from the smoke-laden centre of the world's largest city. Professional medical opinion seemed to endorse the property dealers' hype by favouring the establishment of hospitals, hostels and nursing homes in St John's Wood and Maida Vale. The high walls characteristic of so many villa properties also conferred a degree of privacy favoured by the relatives of those suffering particularly distressing afflictions. A private mental asylum was already established in Melina Place as early as 1830.

HOSPITALS

It was perhaps its then remoteness which favoured the location of a 'Lock Hospital', for the treatment of sexually transmitted diseases and the moral reformation of their victims, at the western edge of what would become Maida Vale in the 1840s. Another specialist institution was the Hospital and Home for Incurable Children, which was located at 2 Maida Vale in the 1890s. By the same decade an Avenue Road residence, originally called *Sunnyside*, had become St Columba's Hospital and

41. *The Hospital of St John and Elizabeth in Grove End Road.*

in the same thoroughfare, at no. 7 stood an establishment for 'Home Treatment of Disease by Diet' and nearby at no. 12 a Yoga School.

In 1901 the Hospital of St John and St Elizabeth moved into new premises in Grove End Road featuring a fine chapel designed by Goldie, an architect who specialised in designing Roman Catholic churches. The hospital was originally located in Great Ormond Street, where it had been founded in 1856 by four Sisters of Mercy on their return from the Crimean War where they had been nursing as part of Florence Nightingale's team.

What became the Maida Vale Hospital for Nervous Diseases was founded in 1866 by a German immigrant, Julius Althaus (1833-1900), as 'The London Infirmary for Epilepsy and Paralysis'. Althaus was one of three brothers who fled to England as refugees from Prussian political repression. His brother Friedrich became a friend of T.H. Huxley and John Tyndall and a professor at University College, London. Julius himself befriended the poet Mathilde Blind and published over fifty books in English on medical subjects.

The Infirmary's first premises, a modest house at 19 Charles Street (now Blandford Place), Marylebone, were too small to admit in-patients; even so over 1,100 out-patient treatments were recorded in its first year of operation. In 1872 the hospital moved into much larger premises, Winterton House, Portland Terrace, overlooking the north side of Regent's Park. It was here that medical history was made in 1884 when surgeon Sir Rickman Godlee (1849-1925) performed the first operation to remove a brain tumour. The patient survived the operation itself but died within the month of post-operative infection. Despite the inevitable disappointment raised by this setback the occasion was still regarded as a sufficiently epoch-making event in medical history to merit a jubilee dinner at the Dorchester fifty years later.

Enthusiastically assisted in its fund-raising by Canon Duckworth of St Mark's, the hospital expanded its facilities and pioneered new therapies involving the use of electricity and massage. By 1897 it was treating 101 in-patients and recording almost 12,000 out-patient attendances in a year. Five years later the hospital moved into new premises at 3 and 4 Maida Vale, although these were not completed until 1913. During the First World War the hospital created a special unit for dealing with neurological casualties from the Royal Flying Corps. The 'Home for Recovery' in which it was housed was actually located at Golders Green. New inter-war developments included ventures into child psychiatry, occupational therapy and postgraduate teaching and pioneering research into electroencephalography. Despite suffering severe damage from a high-explosive bomb in 1940, the hospital kept up its out-patient service throughout the Second World War. It was subsequently merged with the National Hospital for Nervous Diseases and the Institute of Neurology as part of the general reorganisation which established the National Health Service.

RESIDENTIAL INSTITUTIONS

At his death Russian ambassador Count Simon Woronzow (1744-1832), who seemingly preferred Marylebone to his native Moscow, left £500 for the parish poor of Marylebone. This was put towards the construction of the almshouses erected in St John's Wood in 1836: Woronzow Road adjoining acknowledges his generous benefaction. The almshouses, originally Gothic in style, were rebuilt in a neo-Georgian mode in 1965.

Many other residential institutions have been located in the St John's Wood and Maida Vale area. These have included a House of Rest for Christian Workers, which stood at the corner of Finchley Road and Queen's Terrace, the London Female Dormitory for single females of modest means, established in 1859 in Abbey Road and a Phoenix Home for blind women in Alma Square. The 1893 Ordnance Survey map of the area shows a large Home and Orphanage attached to St Augustine's church, Kilburn Park Road, a Queen Victoria Orphanage in Shirland Road and a Home for Female Orphans on St John's Wood Road.

43. The House of Rest at 10 Finchley Road.

42. Design for the St Marylebone Almshouses, then in the process of building in 1836, in St John's Wood Terrace . A part of their cost was donated by Count Woronzow, who is commemorated in nearby Woronzow Road. The architects were John Pink and John St. Erlam

44. The 1878 interior of what became, in 1890, the House of Rest for Christian Workers. It stood at the corner of Finchley Road and Queen's Terrace.

45. *'Pay Day' at St Marylebone Almshouses in St John's Wood Terrace.*

PRIVATE EDUCATIONS

School attendance did not become compulsory in England until 1880. Before then educational provision depended largely on religious, charitable or private initiatives. The inhabitants of St John's Wood at mid-century could not complain of a lack of choice. The Church of England St. John's National School and Infant School in Charles (now Charlbert) Street were intended primarily for the offspring of the humbler classes dwelling in Portland Town. More affluent local residents who wanted their children educated within walking distance would have opted for one of the private institutions with which the area was so abundantly provided. A trawl through Kelly's *Street Directory* for the single year 1849 reveals that there were four establishments designating themselves as just plain 'school' plus two styled as 'preparatory school', three as 'boarding school', four as 'academy' and five even more grandly as 'seminary'. Seven more were specifically designated as a 'ladies' school' and four more as a 'ladies' academy'. Most of these private establishments were run by ladies and known by their names. Many of these proprietors were spinsters or widows, possessed of a decent property but often condemned to eke out limited incomes by exploiting their property in some genteel way. Some of these ladies may have been reasonably educated but few were likely to have had any

formal qualifications. The quality of education on offer ranged, therefore, from quite rigorous preparation for more formal instruction and training elsewhere, to the haphazard transmission of polite manners and drawing-room 'accomplishments' all the way down to mere child-minding. The sculptor Alfred Gilbert fondly remembered Miss Sterling's school in Clifton Gardens as "a place of romping and junketing all day with occasional lessons". The Ordnance Survey map of 1868 records that James Alsop was running an 'academy' at 14 Grove Place, while the Misses Caroline and Julia Read had a 'ladies' seminary' at no. 29 and at no. 7 'Professor' and Mrs George Montague offered lessons in dancing. On Hamilton Terrace Mrs Jane Gomoszynska's seminary at no. 31 was rivalled by Mrs Jane Smith's ladies' academy at no. 33. Many of these institutions lasted only a few years and few were in existence for more than a decade. Perhaps this may explain the curious title of a Loudoun Road establishment – the St. John's Wood Temporary College.

Later in the century state-funded institutions were established to serve the locality, such as Maida Vale High School for Girls in Elgin Avenue (its buildings are now occupied by Paddington College). A spirited and imaginative campaign to establish a Polytechnic for North West London adjacent to what is now Paddington Recreation Ground, led by Lord Randolph Churchill and

46. *A Board School group at Barrow Hill School in 1916.*

supported by the Prince of Wales, fizzled out, however, after failing to reach its fund-raising target. Despite the advent of state schools traditional private establishments continued to attract pupils. In 1893 Mrs. F. Rees-Webbe was still running a ladies' college at 75-77 Maida Vale, while her neighbour, the Revd A.R. With, MA presided over the Vale School at no. 80.

SPECIAL NEEDS AND SPECIALISED INSTRUCTION

The Clergy Orphan School was neither a local nor a metropolitan but a national institution, taking its pupils from the entire kingdom. Of the 130 pupils under instruction there in 1833 only six were from London. Founded in 1749, it originally consisted of a boys' school in Acton and a girls' establishment in Chapel Street, Lisson Green. In 1812 they came together to occupy the new, purpose-built premises in St John's Wood Road, adjacent to the Chapel. The boys, who were educated to the age of fourteen, subsequently moved out, to Canterbury, in 1852. The girls, educated to sixteen, remained until 1895, when

they relocated to Bushey and the school site was purchased by Lord's for an extension to the cricket ground. A similar, but perhaps somewhat less genteel, establishment was the Female Orphan School of Industry in Grove Road. Vocational skills were also stressed at the London Society's Blind School, established in Avenue Road in 1838; here pupils mastered basket-weaving and the skill of repairing cane-bottomed chairs, as well as learning to read from raised letters. The school evidently met a great need and was enlarged in 1864 and again in 1878 and 1912.

The St John's Wood School of Art was founded in 1878 by A.A. Calderon, architect son of artist Philip Calderon (see p. 107). Writing in 1913, A.M. Eyre made the rather curious observation that, upon graduating from its premises in Elm Tree Road, "the advanced student is fitted to take his place in the art world, thoroughly equipped in technical training and with his personality unscathed". However, of an elite eleven 'prominent artists trained in these schools' that Eyre carefully listed, not one subsequently merited an entry in the *Encyclopaedia of British Art* or *The Oxford Companion to Art*, and nor did the School itself, al-

47. *Faculty and students at the St John's Wood Art School. Women figure prominently.*

though Herbert Draper (1863-1920), one of Eyre's selected pantheon, did attract much approval with his 1898 painting of *The Fall of Icarus*. After graduation Draper lived locally at 15 Abbey Road. The School's graduates did also include Ivon Hitchens (*see* p.106), Meredith Frampton (*see* p.106) and Hannah Gluck (*see* p.129). By the 1950s the former premises of the School had become the Constance Spry Flower Arranging School.

48. *The St John's Wood Art School in Elm Tree Road.*

Mr Lord's Ground

The Cambridge Illustrated Dictionary of British Heritage defines Lord's simply as "the most famous cricket ground in the world". As early as 1851 the Rev. James Pycroft, author of *The Cricket Field*, declared confidently that "Of course, *Elysium* means Lord's".

The first written rules for cricket date from 1727. The Marylebone Cricket Club was founded exactly sixty years later, in effect as an offshoot of the White Conduit Club, founded in 1752, which played at Pentonville, near Islington. Cricket had by then spread from its cradle in the villages of Hampshire and Kent to the metropolis itself. Thomas Lord (1755-1832), a Yorkshireman of Scottish descent, employed by the MCC as a bowler and groundsman, was backed by the Earl of Winchilsea and Charles Lennox, future Duke of Richmond, to secure a ground for the new club, which was initially located where Dorset Square now stands. That area was on the northern side of the 'New Road', which had been laid out in 1756 as London's first by-pass and at that time still marked the rough boundary of the built-up area of Marylebone. The location proved immediately popular, some two thousand spectators attending one of the earliest matches. Refreshments were supplied from tents and a batten fence ensured that those who did not pay could not see. The first match played by the MCC under that name took place in 1788, when they defeated and thereafter eclipsed the old White Conduit Club. In 1805 Eton played Harrow at the new ground in what was to become a celebrated annual fixture; Byron was on the losing, Harrow side. The first Gentlemen *vs* Players fixture took place the following year but did not become an annual event until 1819. (The last such match was played in 1962.)

In 1808 Edward Hayward Budd, a mighty smiter of the ball, smashed a delivery right out of the ground and through the glass roof of a greenhouse. When it had been suggested to him that his ground was too small Lord had offered twenty guineas to any batsman who could sky a ball out of it. Budd's feat, however, prompted in Lord a complete and financially convenient loss of memory.

In 1808 Lord was forewarned of a sharp rent rise intended by his new ground landlord, Edward Berkeley Portman, who was more of a businessman and less of a cricket enthusiast than the by now deceased Duke of Dorset had been. In 1809 therefore Thomas Lord dug up his turf and relocated half a mile northwards at North Bank, having

49. *Thomas Lord.*

rented Brick Field and Great Field from the Eyre estate. It was, however, the St John's Wood Cricket Club which first made regular use of this new facility. The MCC played on at Dorset Square until 1811, then played only away fixtures until taking possession of North Bank in 1813. A year later, after a mere three MCC fixtures had been played there, Lord was forced to move yet again as the line of the new Regent's Canal drove straight through the new ground. Once again the famous turf was lifted, although on this occasion at least Lord had the satisfaction of £4,000 compensation from the promoters of the canal. The *new* new ground, on an eighty year lease, was laid out on farmland just north-east of Punker's Barn. Its creation involved filling in a pond whose vestigial presence was to cause drainage problems for generations of ground staff to come. That the club survived these disruptions was due both to the perseverance of Lord himself and to the commitment of such members as Benjamin Ainslabie, its first secretary, a wine merchant who tipped the scales at twenty stones, and George Osbaldestone, 'the sporting squire'.

The first match played at Lord's, on 22 June 1814, was auspiciously marked by a crushing

50. 'The Laws of the Noble Game of Cricket as revised by the Club at St Mary-le-bone' in 1809.

victory over a Hertfordshire side, defeated by an innings and 27 runs. The MCC side included the Revd Lord Frederick Beauclerk, Osbaldestone, the six-hitting Budd and William Ward, who was already a director of the Bank of England, although only 32 years old.

The MCC's occupation of its third and final home occurred in the same year as the consecration of St John's Wood Church. The refreshments on the latter occasion were organised by Thomas Lord, who was a vestryman, and served from the pavilion of his new ground.

A handbill for one of the first major contests organised at 'LORD's NEW Cricket Ground' announced a two-day match between 'TWO SELECT ELEVENS of all ENGLAND', 'The WICKETS to be Pitched at ELEVEN o' Clock' on 20 June 1815. Admittance was charged at sixpence, a modest sum considering that the teams were playing for an advertised wager of 'One Thousand Guineas a Side'. Spectators were promised good stabling but banned from bringing their dogs. Those coming by carriage were advised to drive 'along the New Road through Upper Baker Street or the Road opposite Mary-le-Bone Work-house'. A marquee, capable of holding one hundred, was also available for hire. Nor did Mr Lord miss the opportunity to remind potential patrons that they

could purchase, either at the ground or at his house in 'Upper Gloster Street' 'The Cricket Laws, Bats, Balls and Stumps'. (Lord moved to a newly-built house in St John's Wood Road, overlooking the pitch, at the north-east corner of the ground, in 1816.) Both teams, as usual at this period, consisted of a mixture of patricians and plebeians (i.e. professionals). One was led by Beauclerk and contained one 'Honourable', three 'Esquires' and a 'Junior'. The other was led by a baronet and contained six 'Esquires', including the celebrated 'Squire Osbaldestone '.

Beauclerk dominated the English game for three decades. A son of the Duke of St Albans and a descendant of Nell Gwynne, he was hailed in Lord's centenary history as "the greatest name" in the history of the Club and "the finest all-round gentleman-player in England for many years". A cunning slow bowler, he also made eight centuries at Lord's. He was, however, invariably autocratic as a captain, frequently impetuous at the crease and easily provoked to loss of self-control. His arrogance even extended to hanging a gold watch from the stumps, defying any bowler to hit it, though he was gamesman enough to assure himself of the level of ability he was contending with before risking his timepiece. Reckoning his annual income from cricket at £600 – three years' rental

51. *An 1837 view of sheep trimming the Lord's pitch. In practice, they used herds, hundreds strong, on their way to slaughter at Smithfield.*

on a plush suburban villa – he rarely found time in the season to earn his stipend as vicar of St Alban's by actually preaching a sermon there.

George Osbaldeston – 'Squire of England' – achieved the bowler's supreme triumph of taking ten wickets in an innings and once helped win a match at Lord's while playing with a broken shoulder. This was entirely in character. A fine shot, a brilliant horseman and an outstanding athlete, he once beat the French and Italian real tennis champions, using only his gloved hand, and on another occasion won a wager of 1,000 guineas by riding 200 miles in ten hours – with seventy-eight minutes in hand. At 66 he went 72 hours without sleep in a billiards marathon and at nearly eighty, confined to a bathchair with gout, he won a bet for a sovereign that he could sit for an entire day without moving. He died at 2 Grove Road in 1866, having moved there in 1818 to be near the new ground.

The first decade at Lord's was marked by major milestones in the history of the game. E.H. Budd made the first century at Lord's in 1816, playing against a side captained by Osbaldestone. In 1817 the dimensions of the wicket were standardised at their present size. From 1819 onwards the Gentlemen *vs* Players match became an annual fixture. In 1820 banker William Ward, a future MP for the City of London, scored 278, the first recorded double century, which remained a Lord's record until 1925. In 1822 John Willes, playing for Kent, was no-balled for bowling with a round arm. Willes, in a theatrical gesture, stalked off the field, rode away and never played first-class cricket again; but he had sounded the death-knell of the traditional underarm delivery. Round-arm bowling was finally accepted in 1827, the year in which the annual Oxford *vs* Cambridge match began.

Ward and Willes both *made* cricketing history. Cricketing history was *lost* on 30 July 1825 when the Assembly, Betting and Dressing Rooms burned down, destroying all the MCC's irreplaceable records and trophies, as well as "a large and valuable stock of wine" and all the members 'cricketing apparatus'. How a fire started in the middle of the night has never been satisfactorily

52. *Spectators at the Eton vs Harrow match; from The Graphic 1871. A few seem to be watching the cricket.*

53. *The Gentlemen vs Players match at Lords c.1855.*

explained, as the only heating to be found there during the summer was a candle used for lighting cigars. The conflagration happened almost immediately after William Ward had negotiated the sale of the ground from Lord for £5,000, Lord having obtained permission to build seven pairs of houses on it to provide for his retirement. Ten years later Ward reassigned the lease of the ground to James Henry Dark, brother of Benjamin Dark, a cricket-bat maker of St John's Wood Road, in return for £2,000 and an annuity of £425. In 1860 the freehold came onto the market but, despite Dark's urging, the membership baulked at paying £7,000 for it. The freehold was eventually purchased just six years later for £18,313, the money being advanced by William Nicholson. He was reimbursed from a fund created between 1888 and 1892 by offering life membership of the club to subscribers putting up £100.

The 1825 pavilion disaster did nothing to jeopardise the club's generally acknowledged status as the guardian of the game, which expanded into a role as the governing body of the sport worldwide until the establishment of the Cricket Council in 1970. What would now be called first-class fixtures were first published in the annual *Complete List of all the Grand Matches* compiled by the MCC's official scorer, Samuel Britcher. And it was perhaps a precocious sense of tradition that ensured that, despite the invention of the lawnmower in 1830, Lord's clung to the time-honoured method of keeping the pitch down for another two decades. According to Sir Henry Ponsonby-Fane, the club's Hon. Treasurer : "The grass was never mowed. It was usually kept down by a flock of sheep which was penned up on match-days, and on Saturdays four or five hundred were driven on to the ground on their way to the Monday Smithfield Market."

Perhaps the system was less perfect than pastoral because in 1859 Surrey refused to play on the ground on account of its rough state and in 1863 Sussex made a similar objection. By then 'Players' were becoming known as 'Professionals', and were evidently behaving as such, though not until the 1880s would 'Gentlemen' become known as 'amateurs'.

Half a century after moving to St John's Wood the MCC launched an appeal among its 775 members for mementos and memorabilia for a Cricket Memorial Gallery. In the same year, 1865, the first practice nets were set up and in 1867 a grandstand and press stand were built. Lord's Tavern was rebuilt in 1868 (and again in 1966). In 1869 the club purchased the pavilion which had been erected with a private box on top for the exclusive use of the Prince of Wales. It also bought

54. *England vs Australia at Lords, 1884. Oil by R. Ponsonby Staples. Edward VII (then Prince of Wales) is in the centre of spectators.*

55. *Plan of Lord's Cricket Ground in 1891.*

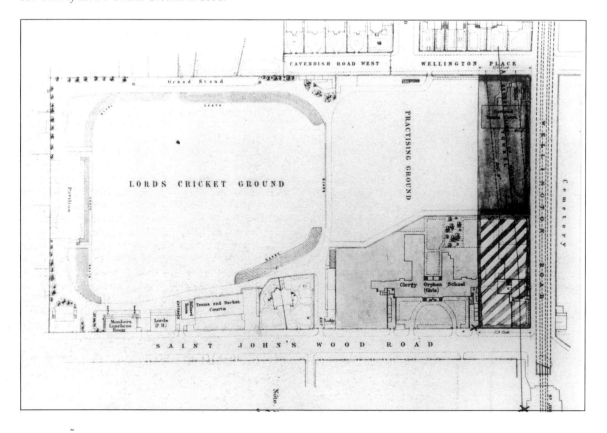

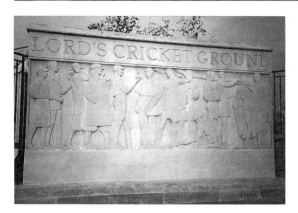

56. *Gilbert Bayes' 1934 relief shows many sports, not just cricket. A cricketer holds up an urn symbolic of the legenday 'Ashes'.*

57. *Plaque erected at Lord's to the memory of W.G. Grace.*

the plot known as Guy's Garden which served as a carriage-stand. W.G. Grace was elected to membership that same year. In 1870 the heavy roller was introduced and in 1872, the year in which Thomas Hearne was appointed head of the ground staff, a tarpaulin was used for the first time to protect the wicket from heavy rain. In 1877 Lord's became the home of Middlesex Cricket Club.

By 1880 membership had expanded to 2,514. These developments prompted a further expansion of facilities. In the 1882 North Terrace was built to hold 2,000 spectators, and houses in Elm Tree Road, St John's Wood Road and Grove End Road were bought up as they became available; and in 1887 Henderson's Nursery was bought from the Clergy Orphan Corporation as a practice ground for £18,500. In 1889-90 the pavilion was rebuilt by Thomas Verity and the Mount Stand was built. By 1903 there were over 5,000 members of the MCC – and 9,000 further candidates for admission. By the time of its Centenary Match in 1914 – when MCC (161) celebrated by defeating Hertfordshire (79 & 55) once more by the exact same margin, an innings and twenty-seven runs – Lord's could accommodate some 30,000 spectators and the original eight acres had been expanded to twenty. In 1923 gates designed by Sir Herbert Baker were installed in honour of the legendary Grace and in 1934 a stone relief in celebration of sport, designed by Gilbert Bayes

and sponsored by Alderman David Isaacs, was unveiled on Wellington Road. (Bayes had also designed the processional cross used in services from 1926 onwards at St Mark's, Hamilton Terrace.)

Lord's connection with Test cricket dates back to its origins. In 1878 the first Australian team to visit England dismissed a powerful MCC side for 52, one bowler taking nine wickets for seventeen runs. The visitors then scored the requisite 53 without losing a man, completing the entire massacre in four and a half hours. England did, however, beat Australia in the first official Test in 1884. Lord's also witnessed the first Tests played by teams from the West Indies (1928), New Zealand (1931), India (1932) and Pakistan (1954). On a more exotic note, in 1844 Lord's hosted an encampment of 'Ioway' Indians who gave demonstrations of their prowess at archery and spirited exhibitions of tribal dancing. In the same year it also played the role of a 'community facility' by accommodating a fair to raise funds for the relief of 'Shipwrecked Fishermen'.

58. *The Eyre Arms Tavern in 1820, located at the junction of Grove End Road and Finchley Road. It was demolished in 1928 to make way for the flats called Eyre Court.*

Leisure and Pleasure

AN INSTANT SUCCESS

The Eyre Arms Tavern flourished from its very opening in 1821. Built to high specifications – Thomas Smith in 1833 referred to it warmly as "this splendid edifice" – the Tavern could accommodate some 1,500 people. In terms of location it benefited not only from being beside a major thoroughfare out of the capital but also from serving as the terminus of the prestigious Atlas omnibus service which ran, via the City, all the way to Camberwell. From the roof of the building, a favourite venue for a reflective pipe and pint, it was possible to look out over Regent's Park to the distant prospect of the dome of St. Paul's. Indoor attractions included a boxing club, concerts, improving lectures by intellectuals, such as Thackeray, and rather less improving plays with titles like *The Modern Vampire* and *Castle Spectre*.

To the rear of the Eyre Arms were "extensive grounds laid out with great taste and effect", suitable for crowd-pulling entertainments.

The entertainments did not always work out as planned. In July 1836 the artist C. R. Leslie took a group of children to see a tight-rope walker there. Unfortunately the rope proved to be not sufficiently tight enough, with the result that the female acrobat undertaking the aerial odyssey found herself marooned amidst a distracting cascade of fireworks. She was eventually rescued by an ex-sailor in the crowd who gamely climbed a ladder which was itself balanced on top of a table. On the evening of 7 June 1838 Mr. John Hampton entered on what proved to be a similarly perilous enterprise in his patriotically named new balloon 'The Albion'. Unfortunately for him the car hanging under the balloon first struck some poles erected for a firework display and then crashed into the gable of a house before depositing the intrepid aeronaut some five hundred yards from his starting-point "in the grounds of Mr. Cook, a market gardener, situated at the end of Wellington Place". It was in the grounds of the

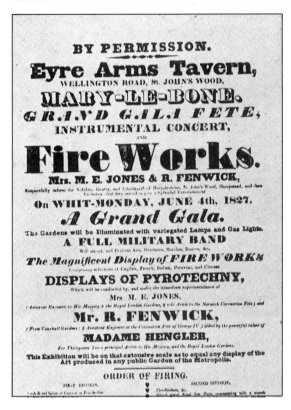

Eyre Arms that rehearsals for the Eglinton tournament (see pp.64-5) were organised the following year – but at least that turned out to be a fiasco rather than a near-disaster. The Eyre Arms Assembly Rooms were later upgraded to become the Wellington Hall – "decorated in the Florentine style and lighted by electricity, whilst the floor is on roller springs and is acknowledged to be perfect for the exercise of the terpsichorean art.". The grounds were eventually built over to become a riding-school and the Eyre Arms itself was finally demolished in 1928 to make way for the construction of Eyre Court.

AN INSTANT DISASTER

The magnificent hostelry now known as Crocker's Folly, which stands in Aberdeen Place, was the product of an optimism which was literally misplaced. Learning of the approach of the Great Central Railway, Frank Crocker sank a fortune into erecting 'The Crown Hotel', which he confidently expected to prove a goldmine, being located right opposite the supposed site of the new terminus of the line. The hotel opened in 1892, complete with coffered ceilings, baronial fireplaces, marble columns and bar-counters and not one, but two, full-sized billiard-tables. Unfortunately the line actually terminated in Marylebone itself and

59. *A grand firework display at the Eyre Arms in 1827.*

60. *The Eyre Arms c.1906. The Wellington Assembly Hall has been added.*

61. Crocker's Folly in 1998.

62. The Knights of St John pub - in which the St John's Wood Art Club was launched.

63. Arthur Hacker drawing Alma-Tadema's silhouette on the wall of the pub dining room. It was not appreciated by the landlord and it was wiped off.

Crocker terminated out of an upstairs window. His legacy, however, now thrives.

THE ST JOHN'S WOOD ART CLUB

This Club was founded in December 1894 at a meeting held in the home of the artist Walter Dendy Sadler, who served as its first secretary. John Burgess R.A. was the first treasurer. Of the nine others present on that occasion the most eminent was the architect Charles Voysey. An inaugural Club dinner was held in an upper room at The Knights of St John pub on 30 January 1895, where the chair was taken by the sculptor Alfred Gilbert; Onslow Ford was also present. Arthur Hacker RA enlivened the proceedings by drawing Alma-Tadema in silhouette on the wall – "this priceless transcript" being subsequently white-washed over by the landlord. Such a Philistine gesture may in part explain the Club's decision of November 1895 to move to more spacious premises at the Eyre Arms, where they had their own ground floor room, use of two billiard tables from five until eight every evening, and the opportunity to organise suppers in the imposing surroundings of the Wellington Rooms. Their other activities included discussion evenings and smoking concerts, at which musically gifted honorary members performed. An Artistic Copyright

64. *The interior of the St John's Wood Art Club in the former home of the writer, Tom Hood. Note the frieze of members' portraits. Drawing by Cecil King.*

Committee, chaired by Alma-Tadema, worked usefully to promote members' professional interests. In 1900 the Club took over the studio, sitting-rooms and basement of the Finchley Road house once occupied by the writer Thomas Hood. Ninety-two of the Club's by then 111 members were present for an inaugural supper in their new premises. Later their portraits would become a frieze adorning the walls of the club's spacious sitting-room. Guests of the Club included such Edwardian celebrities as the writer G. K. Chesterton and Baden-Powell, the hero of Mafeking and founder of the Boy Scouts.

FLIGHT OF THE ARROW

Archery, banished from the battlefield by the emergence of firearms, was revived as a genteel sport under the aegis of the Toxophilite Society in 1781. The Prince Regent gave his personal patronage to what became 'the Royal Tox' and at one stage its ground was located in Regent's Park. Archery was almost unique among recreations in the early nineteenth century in being considered not only fashionable but also a pastime in which both sexes could participate. It therefore afforded a welcome opportunity among the respectable classes for socialising and discreet flirtation. In 1874 W. P. Frith painted a study *The Fair Toxophilites* in which he used three of his own daughters as the models. A commercial directory of mid-century affirms the popularity of the sport by listing no less than fourteen 'archery warehouses' in the central London area, eight of them concentrated around Oxford Street, Tottenham Court Road and Bloomsbury, to the south of Regent's Park. In St. John's Wood the Abbey Tavern on Violet Hill had its own archery ground but this, being attached to a public house, was presumably less respectable than the St Marylebone Archery Ground in Marlborough Place. With the rise of tennis as an alternative mixed-sex recreation from the 1870s onwards this facility metamorphosed to become the Marlborough Lawn Tennis Ground and later changed again to become the Victoria Rifle Ground. It was finally built over after 1939.

65. *An advertisement for archery at the rear of the Abbey Tavern in 1844. The foreground is now covered by Abbey Gardens and the houses on the right are in Hamilton Terrace.*

PADDINGTON RECREATION GROUND

A plan drawn up in 1840 by George Gutch, architect to the diocese of London, envisaged covering the entire Maida Vale area with streets of houses. Development was far slower than originally envisaged but by the 1880s local cricket enthusiasts had become acutely aware that fields they had habitually used for matches were everywhere disappearing to make way for building. Representatives of several clubs, led by the Paddington Cricket Club, therefore met and resolved that "steps should immediately be taken to secure for Paddington a ground available for cricket and other forms of outdoor recreation". Their target location was the as yet open land between Shirland Road and Portsdown Road (now Randolph Av-

enue), which had already been used for sports by the employees of Liberty's and Whiteley's department stores. On 7 July 1887 what had temporarily become the Paddington Cricket Club ground, held on a personal lease by its Secretary, R. M. Beachcroft, was the scene of extensive junketings – music, Punch and Judy, fireworks – in honour of Queen Victoria's Golden Jubilee, attended by 1,500 elderly residents of the locality and some 8,500 schoolchildren, each of whom was presented with a souvenir mug. The following winter proved somewhat less joyous, being accompanied by such severe unemployment that a local committee convened by Lord Randolph Churchill (1849-95), then M.P. for South Paddington, raised a relief fund of £1,800 to pay for public works. The en-

66. *Rear view of the gardens of the Abbey Tavern. Artist and date unknown.*

67. *The Warrington Hotel, one of the most impressive public houses in the area.*

terprising Beachcroft saw in this well-intentioned, but as yet unfocused, initiative a golden opportunity. In exchange for his willingness to rent, at his own personal risk, another eleven acres adjacent to the nine-acre cricket ground he had already laid out at his own expense, the Relief Fund would pay for men to drain, fence and landscape the additional area, which was currently disfigured by heaps of hardcore and spoil dumped by local contractors. Five hundred men thus found ten weeks paid work in removing 35,000 yards of clay, 2,800 yards of ballast and 40,000 loads of rubbish and laying down 1,300 yards of ashes. The outcome of their labours included tennis courts, cinder cycling and running tracks and a fine pavilion, not to mention The Mound, a landscape feature created from the detritus which had not been carted

away elsewhere. A Beachcroft Gate and Churchill Gate perpetuated the memory of the men who made it all possible,

One of the nearby area's most interesting features was London's first (1875) concrete roller-skating rink, established in a corrugated iron building in Portsdown Road. When the roller-skating craze waned it was converted to become London's first covered winter tennis-courts.

The Maida Vale Skating Palace and Club in Delaware Road was licensed in the period 1909-1912 to seat 2,620 persons. By 1913 it had been converted into offices from which the newly established National Insurance scheme was administered. In 1934 it was converted yet again to become a BBC rehearsal studio for orchestral concerts and opera.

68. Plan of Paddington Recreation Ground in 1901.

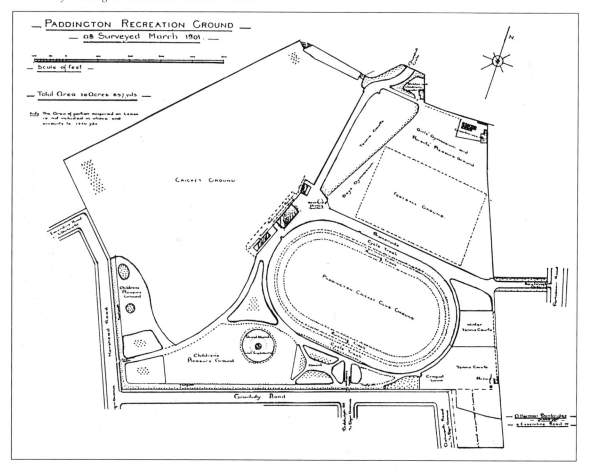

THE PADDINGTON BOWLING & SPORTS CLUB
CASTELLAIN ROAD, MAIDA VALE, W.9.

69. *Paddington Bowling and Sports Club at the Paddington Recreation Ground.*

70. *Maida Vale Skating Palace, claimed as 'the largest rink in the world', 500 feet long and 110 feet wide.*

MAIDA VALE SKATING PALACE & CLUB, LONDON.
THE LARGEST RINK IN THE WORLD.
500 FEET LONG, 110 FEET WIDE.
STEELWORK DESIGNED, MANUFACTURED AND ERECTED BY
JOHN BOOTH & SONS, BOLTON, ENGLAND.

Behind High Walls

On being informed that the philosopher Herbert Spencer had gone to live in St John's Wood a bishop is said to have responded by asking "And who is the lady?" The association was, apparently, virtually automatic, even for bishops. In *The Man of Property* (1906) John Galsworthy described Jolyon Forsyte visiting his son in St. John's Wood – "he looked about him with interest; for this was a district which no Forsyte entered without open disapproval and secret curiosity". When he left he found himself walking "between little rows of houses, all suggesting to him (erroneously no doubt but the prejudices of a Forsyte are sacred) shady histories of some sort or kind." And, writing just a few years later, local historian Alan Montgomery Eyre asserted that "Whatever other titles to fame St John's Wood possesses surely its last surviving association will be that with the heroines of passion and the victims of propriety. "

71. *Mrs Meeres' house in Loudoun Road.*

RESTORATION AND REGENCY

Even before high walls offered the possibility of privacy for unorthodox liaisons, it was its relative remoteness that appears to have made St John's Wood an attractive location in which to establish a mistress. Several examples are believed to date from the Restoration period. Amy Walter, mistress of Lord Fitzhardinge, was living in a cottage near what became Loudoun Road when she learned of his death in a great sea-fight against the Dutch in 1665. In 1678 German-born Mary Moders (alias Stedman, alias Carleton) proclaimed in her last speech at Tyburn, just before she was hanged for theft, that she had once lived "near by Great St John's Wood" as the mistress of a married clergyman. After that she had passed herself off as a princess and committed bigamy – of which charge she managed to get herself acquitted. She then exploited this exploit by playing herself on stage in *The German Princess*, which told her extraordinary story – to the disgust of diarist Samuel Pepys, who saw her at the Duke's Playhouse.

After the Restoration the Regency period is, perhaps, most immediately associated with loose morals at court and among the aristocracy. Mrs Fitzherbert, the Roman Catholic with whom George IV had gone through a form of marriage when he was still Prince of Wales, eventually retired to a life of relative tranquility at Stockleigh House, (Prince) Albert Road. A dwelling at the corner of Loudoun Road and Marlborough Road was likewise the retirement home of Jane Belmont, the same king's last mistress.

Contemporary with these courtly courtesans were Mrs Everest and Molly Meeres. Tall, fair-haired Mrs Everest, a peer's daughter, eloped with a footman then dropped him for a wealthy sugar-broker. When he died just two years later she found herself wealthy in her own right and set up in some style in Circus Road. Mary 'Molly ' Meeres (née Baker), daughter of a Leicester blacksmith, went on the stage at seventeen but quit a promising career to become an adventuress and may have provided Thackeray with the model for his greatest fictional creation, the charmingly amoral Becky Sharp, heroine of *Vanity Fair*. Molly's liaison with an elderly, widowed banker enabled her to settle in Loudoun Road.

In 1812 William Pole Wellesley (1788-1857), 4th Earl of Mornington, married the heiress Catherine Tylney-Long but they soon separated and he commenced a liaison with Helena, the wife of a Captain Thomas Bligh. In 1823 Wellesley, a nephew of the Duke of Wellington, was taken to court by a Mr William Jackson in respect of an alleged trespass and damage to the extent of £350. Judgment was given against Wellesley and the sheriffs took possession of his box at the Theatre Royal, Drury Lane, valued at £600. Shunned by polite Society, in 1826 he took 3 Hall's Place, the largest house in Hall Road. In 1828 he finally married Helena but Society, or at least the *Morning Chronicle*, proved unforgiving and in an obituary published almost thirty years later characterised him as being "redeemed by no single virtue, adorned by no single grace".

DIPLOMACY AND A DOMESTIC DISPUTE

In March 1836 no. 5 Lodge Road was temporarily occupied by M.I. Khan, a 'Mulvi' or learned man, in this case an astronomer, who was representing the King of the Indian princely state of Oudh. Sounds of distress from the high-walled garden of the house were investigated by a Marylebone vestryman (i.e. local councillor) and a member of the Board of Guardians (which was responsible for supervising the poor), accompanied by a fluent speaker of Persian, then the language of diplomacy and courtly discourse in the sub-continent. In the garden of no. 5 they found a female Indian servant, naked but for a tattered rug. Enquiries of the Mulvi's wife raised the allegation that the girl was demented, had been taken into their household as an act of charity and had returned this kindness with insolent disobedience. As she appeared to have been flogged, half-scalped and starved in punishment she was immediately transferred to the parish infirmary. Further enquiries revealed that the Mulvi's wife had already dismissed an English interpreter for allegedly stealing petty cash. His version of events was that he had left because he refused to procure five girls for the Mulvi to take back for his employer's harem. At this point the East India Company, whose employees were fairly thick on the ground in St John's Wood, intervened in the person of Captain Robert Grindlay, formerly of the Bombay Infantry and currently of 35 North Bank. Grindlay accompanied the Mulvi and his wife to Marylebone police court, where the bench was assured that the girl who had been beaten was insane – an explanation that appears to have been satisfactory. At all events the Mulvi was still elected to honorary membership of the Athenaeum and the Travellers' Club – although the East India Company also advised William IV against granting him an audience or accepting his diplomatic gifts. Oudh was subsequently annexed to British control following allegations of tyrannical abuses by its ruler.

AN EMPRESS MANQUÉ

At eighteen Harriet Howard (née Elizabeth Anne Hargett) was installed in a splendid house in Circus Road in "a stable arrangement with all the appearance of a marriage". Her patron was Major Francis Mountjoy Martyn of the Second Life Guards, a handsome, virile fellow whose wife had proved too frail to give him an heir. Harriet should have been gratified to have found such a safe haven. At fifteen she had run away from a respectable home in Great Yarmouth in the company of Jem Mason, a steeplechaser. He promised to get her on the London stage and she did indeed

72. *Harriet Howard, who lived in Circus Road.*

appear at the Haymarket. The play could not have had a more appropriate title – *The Love Chase*. But Harriet was no great talent and Jem soon moved on to pastures new. Harriet at that time is said to have been living in Lodge Road.

Major Martyn gave every evidence of wanting a long-term relationship, settling a large capital sum on Harriet as evidence of his intentions. When she presented him with a son he bought property in London in her name. Harriet's devotion to her benefactor was, however, soon undermined by a chance encounter at Gore House, home of the celebrated hostess, Lady Blessington, where she was introduced to the guest of honour, Prince Louis-Napoleon, nephew of Bonaparte himself. At that time the prince was an exile, with ardent but ill-formed ambitions to re-create his late uncle's realm and put himself at the head of it. The very next morning after their introduction Louis-Napoleon, immediately smitten by Harriet's beauty, rode out to Circus Road and was admitted to her boudoir.

Whether Harriet was as taken with the prince as he was with her, whether she was simply exhilarated by the whiff of conspiracy and intrigue which surrounded him, or whether she even then began to dream of herself as a future empress of France, whatever her motives, she informed Martyn that henceforth she, her son and her fortune would be at the disposal of Louis-Napoleon.

That was in 1838. The house in Circus Road was closed up. Harriet loaned the penniless prince large sums that he badly needed. And stuck by him. In 1851 he finally seized power in a *coup d'état* and did, indeed, make himself emperor. Harriet, for all her looks, loyalty and generosity, was, however, deemed not to be empress material and was duly side-lined to the Château Beauregard, with a title to match, and an allowance to support both. The emperor married a haughty Spanish princess and Harriet died at her château, embittered, aged forty-five.

A GALLIC PASSION

To his English contemporaries there was something indefinably louche about the superbly executed snapshots of smart society painted by James (actually Jacques-Joseph) Tissot (1836-1902) during more than a decade of residence in England. Ruskin's dismissal of his works as "mere coloured photographs" was at least a backhanded acknowledgment of their technical virtuosity. Tissot had, after all, studied at the École des Beaux Arts under Ingres, a master of polish and precision.

Tissot's personal manner – at once languid and mischievous – seemed to affirm the stereotype of the philandering French artist, coolly appraising each pretty girl he passed on the street, more as a matter of reflex than routine. When he painted women, even though their bodies were entirely concealed by the fripperies and finery of the fussy fashions of the 1870s, Tissot somehow contrived to convey what they would look like with much less, or indeed, nothing on. Where other artists might have felt tempted to expose, Tissot was content to insinuate. Like his friend Whistler, Tissot was fascinated by London's great river. A picture he exhibited at the Royal Academy in 1876, innocently entitled *The Thames*, focuses on a sailor out with two girls for a pleasure-boat trip through the docks. Their lounging postures and rumpled

73.   *James Tissot's Holyday, c.1876.*

clothes, flashy but unkempt at the same time, the champagne bottle they are sharing and, glimpsed behind them, the brazen bare bosom of a ship's figurehead, all added up to a composition which *The Graphic* pronounced to be "hardly nice in its suggestions. More French, shall we say, than English?"

Unlike fellow refugees Monet and Pissarro, Tissot had actually seen action in the Franco-Prussian war (1870-71) and been involved in the revolutionary Commune, before fleeing to London. Unlike them also he did not return to France once hostilities ceased. Instead he settled his beautiful Irish mistress and favourite model, Kathleen Newton, and her children, with her married sister, Mrs Hervey, in Hill Road and initially lived himself in Springfield Road but then moved to 17 (afterwards 34, now 44) Grove End Road. Here he flamboyantly embellished the garden with a pool and pseudo-Roman arcade which provided a striking backdrop for many of his paintings. Despite his roving eye Tissot was devoted to the flame-haired Kathleen and when she died from tuberculosis at the age of 28 both his idyll and his

composure were shattered for ever. Abandoning both St John's Wood and his accustomed subject-matter, he returned to France and reverted to the intense religiosity of his early youth. Most of his later life was dedicated to producing vast numbers of etchings of Biblical scenes, based on first-hand observations made in the course of three lengthy visits to Palestine. These brought him *immense* wealth but little contentment.

THE SPORTING EARL

After Lady Grace Gordon, wife of Hugh Cecil, 5th Earl of Lonsdale (1857-1944), miscarried, he took his favours elsewhere, and most consistently with Violet Cameron, whom he installed at 37 Acacia Road. Lonsdale gained much notoriety by knocking out the American heavyweight champion John L. Sullivan, and she gained not a little by 'knocking out ' a daughter for him.

His gratitude was expressed not merely by keeping her and the child in some style but also by supporting her opera company. He could afford it, having an annual income of £200,000, mostly

74. Faded Arcadia: 44 Grove End Road in 1998.

75. *Acacia Road, home of Violet Cameron, at the turn of this century.*

from coal mines. After all, he was reputed to spend £3,000 a year on cigars alone. Edward VII complimented him backhandedly as "... almost an Emperor, but not *quite* a gentleman." In 1905 Lonsdale became the first president of the Automobile Association which adopted yellow, the colour of the Lonsdale livery, for its badges. His name is perpetuated in that great boxing trophy, the Lonsdale belt.

TARTS WITH TARTS

It has been observed that other people's tastes in sex are often as incomprehensible as other people's tastes in food. Frederick Cooper, also known as 'the Minotaur', managed to combine the two during his visits to the home of one Watson, tenant of 2 Boscobel Place, Alpha Road. Here, accompanied by a basket of his favourite ammunition, he took possession of a former schoolroom and

sat on the floor, pelting undraped ladies with jam tarts as they cavorted around him. What A. M. Eyre was later to call this "singular and rather revolting exhibition" was not long to be kept secret and proved too much even for the normally complaisant residents of St John's Wood. They murmured. They complained. They came round to remonstrate with the Watsons. As they came to the front door so Cooper left by the back. Although he dared not return to the Watsons he continued to visit the Wood to indulge in his particular diversion, employing other ladies at other addresses. The Minotaur died in 1897, having left the intriguing instruction to his main beneficiary that he could collect his legacy of £30,000 only after his corpse had been cremated, unseen by any other eyes.

The Military

THE PROFESSIONALS

It was in 1804 that drivers and horses of an artillery brigade were first billeted at St John's Wood farm at a rental of £150 per year. In 1810 the arrangement was put on a more permanent footing when a four-acre plot was leased from the Eyre family and a barrack block built. The occupants were moved out in 1819 "in consequence of the peace" but the Board of Ordnance was unable to find a buyer for the remainder of the lease, so in 1823 the Cavalry Riding Establishment was relocated to St John's Wood from Pimlico. A purpose-built riding school, now the oldest surviving part of the barracks complex, was completed in 1825 at a cost of £6,000. The purpose of this establishment was to encourage the development of "one uniform system of equitation" throughout the cavalry, and to this end two or three of the most promising riders were selected from each unit "for the express purpose of being perfected in the method of riding by balance, in imitation of the mode practised by German troops". They were then returned to their units as instructors.

In 1832 the cavalry transferred to Maidstone and the barracks became a Recruit Depot for the Foot Guards, a new barrack block being built in 1835.

(This was finally demolished in 1969.) Reflecting a growing official recognition of the benefits of organised sport the recreational facilities provided for troops included a cricket field and a fives court.

In 1876 the infantry were moved out to make way for cavalry who used St John's Wood as a temporary accommodation while their Knightsbridge quarters were being rebuilt. In 1880 a Horse Artillery Battery moved in on a permanent basis and a cavalry presence has been maintained at St John's Wood ever since. The present barracks complex was completed in 1972, the only old buildings being the riding school and the Officers' Mess.

The current unit known as the King's Troop, Royal Horse Artillery was established on 17 April 1946 at the express wish of King George VI to carry out ceremonial duties in traditional style. In deference to his wishes it has retained its original title despite the change of sovereign since its formation. The King's Troop not only takes responsibility for firing formal salutes in Hyde Park on such occasions as the anniversary of the Queen's accession but also participates in such annual events as the Lord Mayor's Show and the Armistice Day parade, as well as extraordinary occasions, such as royal funerals. The daring Musical Drive performed by a King's Troop contingent is also one of the highlights of the Royal Tournament each year and has been performed before many delighted audiences on both sides of the Atlantic.

76. *The Foot Guards at drill at St John's Wood Barracks. From the Illustrated London News 26 August, 1854, during the Crimean War.*

THE AMATEURS

Unlikely though it may at first sight seem, the members of the St John's Wood Clique of painters (*see* p.107) were also would-be warriors, at least on a part-time basis. Their penchant for dressing up in historical costumes might partly explain their motivation, as might their generally shared appetite for a 'lark' and an expedition into the country. Whatever the reason, most of them joined the Volunteer movement which was inspired in the late 1850s by a somewhat misplaced hysteria about the possibilities of a French invasion. Large numbers of rifle companies were recruited, chiefly from middle-class patriots, to drill and do target practice at weekends and in the evenings. Each summer, rather in the spirit of a Boy Scout camp, they would crowd onto trains to assemble on Wimbledon Common or at Brighton for 'field days' when they would march in dust-shrouded formations and shoot at targets set at a more challenging distance than the length of a local drill-hall. Of the St John's Wood Clique members Wynfield eventually rose to the rank of captain with the Artists' Corps (38th Middlesex Regiment), inducing Yeames and Hodgson, and eventually Calderon and Marks as well, to join the colours. The leading lights of that well-connected unit included its colonel Sir Frederick (later Lord) Leighton, the future President of the Royal Academy (1878-1896), and his polished protégé, the socialite Val Prinsep (1834-1904), who was a captain. The Volunteers never were called upon to oppose the French in anger but the movement lingered on until merged with the yeomanry and militia to form the Territorial Force on the eve of the Great War. Its most notable legacy, at least to the civilian society it was called into being to protect, is the large number of public houses called 'The Volunteer', to many of which, no doubt, parched riflemen repaired for well-earned refreshment after an evening's martial exertions.

FANTASY AND FIASCO

Inspired by the novels of Sir Walter Scott, Archibald Montgomerie, 13th Earl of Eglinton determined to revive the glories of the medieval tournament at his home in Ayrshire. Realising that the requisite martial skills had fallen into desuetude over the course of some three centuries, he therefore organised some preliminary rehearsals, which were held on a patch of ground behind the Eyre Arms Tavern. Sessions were held on Tuesdays and Saturdays and attracted the involvement of a select band of aristocrats and even the exiled Prince Louis-Napoleon. The chief exercise consisted of trying to knock over a dummy knight mounted

77. *Frederick, Lord Leighton; a caricature from Vanity Fair, 1872.*

on a wooden horse, which trundled on rails down an inclined plane. To enhance the muscularity of their unusually exposed legs most of the participants appear to have had recourse to the Covent Garden premises of a Mr Haigh, a theatrical hosier, who supplied them with appropriately stuffed tights. A correspondent of *The Times*, affecting the omniscience proper to that august journal, assured readers in his account of one of these occasions that "there were no serious accidents yesterday, and the whole thing went off as such things usually do". A letter to the editor of that same newspaper warned in mock-seriousness that anyone causing the death of a participant would be guilty of manslaughter and even 'noble dames and demoiselles' among the onlookers would be deemed guilty of aiding and abetting and therefore liable to a fine or imprisonment or both. Undeterred, Eglinton and his cronies continued their preparations until the great day – 28 August

78. A 'Tournament' thought to be in the grounds of the Eyre Arms.

1839, when a huge crowd gathered in Ayrshire to witness the spectacle. As John Steegman observed in his study of *Victorian Taste* "it was magnificently extravagant and not at all utilitarian and it made many earnest people very angry". Doubtless those same people derived much satisfaction from learning that the whole event was quite literally a wash-out as torrents of rain totally drenched both participants and onlookers. The memory of this extraordinary occasion was, however, perpetuated by Landseer, who painted Lord Worcester, the 7th Duke of Beaufort, kitted out as a medieval knight, and by Disraeli who incorporated it in his novel *Endymion* as the Montfort Tournament.

HEROES REMEMBERED

Ordnance Road appropriately perpetuates the name of the original lessee of the St John's Wood barracks, the Board of Ordnance. Marlborough Road and Wellington Road commemorate the fame of two of Britain's greatest commanders. Blenheim Road and Terrace are named for Marlborough's greatest victory; fought at Blindheim in Bavaria, it represented the first decisive defeat of the army of Louis XIV of France in forty years. In contrast to Marlborough and Wellington, the name of Admiral Cochrane (1775-1860), preserved in Cochrane Street (formerly Cochrane Terrace) is,

considering the extraordinary nature of his exploits, less well known than C.S. Forester's 'Captain Hornblower', for whom he might well have supplied the model. As commander of the sloop *Speedy* buccaneering Thomas Cochrane, 10th Earl of Dundonald took over fifty prizes in the years 1800-1801. He later found similar success off the Azores (1805) and the Bay of Biscay (1806), leading Napoleon himself to dub him *'le loup des mers'*. But Cochrane's fearless exposure of abuses in naval administration made him powerful enemies in the hierarchy of command and for long periods he was condemned to the unglamorous task of patrolling the coaling route from Newcastle to London. In 1814 Cochrane was unjustly accused of participation in a stock exchange fraud, allegedly arising from his prior knowledge of the defeat of the French. As a consequence he was fined, imprisoned, expelled from the navy and, having previously been honoured with the Order of the Bath, suffered the humiliation of having his banner kicked down the steps of Westminster Abbey. Thus freed, perforce, of British commitments, Cochrane joined the rush of ex-servicemen who thronged to fight in South America for the independence of Spain and Portugal's former colonies. Having commanded the infant navies of Chile, Peru and Brazil with brilliant success, he went on to command the Greek navy (1827-28) in that country's struggle against Ottoman rule. In these operations Cochrane pioneered the use of steam-propelled ships of war and farsightedly advocated the adoption of the screw propeller. Pardoned, exonerated and reinstated in the navy, he was promoted rear-admiral in 1832 and moved into Hanover Lodge, Regent's Park that same year. Cochrane Street was then hastily named after him, as though in belated recognition of his unjust disgrace. Hanover Lodge, which gave Lodge Road its name, was, appropriately, to be the retirement home of Admiral Beatty, commander of the British fleet at the Battle of Jutland. Cochrane eventually retired as full admiral and was honoured with burial in the very nave of Westminster Abbey.

Townshend Road is named for the commander who received the French surrender at Quebec in 1759, following the death of General Wolfe in the hour of his victory. The name of Maida Vale recalls a long forgotten encounter of the Peninsular War in Spain, when, in 1806, a British force under Sir John Stuart – commemorated in the Hero of Maida public house – crushingly defeated a French force commanded by General Regnier. Nugent Terrace was named for Field-Marshal Sir George Nugent (1757-1849), who lived in St John's Wood in his retirement. Born the illegitimate son of a colonel of the Foot Guards, Nugent fought as a junior officer in the American War of Independence and rose to become commander-in-chief in Jamaica, then in India, as well as serving as a Member of Parliament. His brother, Admiral Sir Charles Nugent (1759-1844) owned property in St John's Wood. Alma Square and Alma Gardens refer to the first major battle of the Crimean War when, in 1854, a combined Franco-British force cleared the way to the Russian strongpoint of Sebastopol, inflicting 6,000 casualties on the enemy.

St John's Wood Burial Ground supplies the last resting-place of a number of military men, many of them with Indian connections. Maj.-Gen. Sir Alexander Caldwell (1763-1839) was commander of the Bengal Artillery. Capt. Francis Henderson of Madras died, ironically, "on his way to embark for England for the restoration of his health". Lt David Henderson and Lt Daniel May were casualties of the great rebellion of 1857. Samuel Godley (1781-1832), however, was one of the heroes of Waterloo; a private in the Second Life Guards, who played a heroic role in the deadly sword fight which followed a charge against the French cuirassiers. His handsome, if slightly obscured, tombstone was raised at the expense of the non-commissioned officers of his former regiment.

79. The memorial to Samuel Godley in St John's churchyard.

80. Memorial in St John's churchyard to military members of the Henderson family.

The Philosophic Mind

SPENCER AT HOME

Charles Darwin once wrote of **Herbert Spencer** (1820-1903) that "I could bear and rather enjoy feeling that he was twice as ingenious and clever as myself but when I feel that he is about a dozen times my superior ... I feel aggrieved". Although Darwin's prose was both elegant and vigorous, it was actually Spencer who coined the phrase most often, and erroneously, attributed to the author of the *Origin of Species* – "the survival of the fittest".

Spencer had even less formal education than Darwin and by seventeen had qualified to work as a railway engineer. Acutely aware that, as he himself recorded, "to play billiards well was the sign of an ill-spent youth", he became, perhaps appropriately for the son of a private tutor, a compulsive autodidact. After dabbling with inventing and writing for progressive periodicals in the provinces, at 28 he became a sub-editor on *The Economist*. An inheritance then enabled him to devote himself to scholarly pursuits, provided he lived fairly frugally as a bachelor. Unencumbered by university training, unrestricted by any academic appointment, Spencer set himself to systematise all knowledge in an intellectual project worthy to rank beside the efforts of Aristotle or Comte in its sheer scale and audacity. The very title of his first major publication gives more than an intimation of what was to follow – *Social Statics or the Conditions essential to Human Happiness specified, and the First of them Developed* (1850). Darwin's theory of evolution subsequently provided the unifying motif of Spencer's unwearying output. Some idea of his style as an author can be gleaned from his definition of evolution as "an integration of matter and concomitant dissipation of motion; during which matter passes from an indefinite incoherent homogeneity to a definite coherent heterogeneity; and during which the retained motion undergoes a parallel transformation." Despite the often forbidding density of his polysyllabic prose Spencer's *Principles of Psychology* (1855) became a set text at Harvard and his *Principles of Biology* (1864-7) a set text at Oxford. His *Study of Sociology* (1873) provided the core around which Yale built the first course on that subject to be offered at an American university.

In the 1850s Spencer lived briefly at 4 St Anne's Terrace, then at 16 Loudoun Road and at 20 Clifton

By courtesy of the National Portrait Gallery

81. *Herbert Spencer; a caricature in Vanity Fair, 1879.*

Road and thereafter at a succession of boarding-houses. It was at one of these in November 1873 that Spencer gave a dinner in his private parlour for John Fiske, a young American polymath on his first trip to England, who was a great devotee of Spencerean ideas. There were 'choice wines' and 'brilliant conversation ' ranging over 'pretty much the whole universe from cellar to attic'. Apart from Spencer himself, whom he found "gentle and admirable as always", the other guests included G.H. Lewes , who "kept us in a roar most of the time" and T.H. Huxley, with whom Fiske was immensely impressed – "handsome as an Apollo ... immensely in earnest – and thoroughly frank and cordial and modest ... such a clean-cut mind ... to see such a man as Huxley is never to forget him".

In 1889 Spencer decided to settle at 64 Avenue Road, which two sisters agreed to furnish, and clean and cook for him, in return for his paying the rent and taxes as well as their wages. One sister described it as "essentially a man's house", lacking "that homelike, comfortable touch which cosy corners and deep window-seats would have done ... great rectangular rooms, blank, staring and wearisome ...". Their principal occupant was no ornament, either. A resident of St John's Wood described Spencer at this period as the great man stood waiting for a bus outside the Eyre Arms – "dressed in curious, ill-fitting garments: one of his trouser-legs being caught above his elastic gaiter boots. His quaint, large-brimmed hat almost rested on his shoulders. He wore enormous spectacles, and his face was clean shaven, save for a luxuriant 'Newgate fringe', snow-white, which covered a pink cravat."

For a Darwinian who had once boldly asserted that "the first requisite to success in life is to be a good animal", the hypochondriac Spencer followed a decidedly wimpish regime of nursery food, and was for ever feeling his own pulse, keeping draughts at bay with numerous rugs and shutting out the trivial chatter of his housekeepers with earplugs. In many ways he must have proved a sore trial, requiring his bed be made with a small bolster under the mattress to fit into the small of his back, insisting that his chair be upholstered in an 'impure purple' which reminded him of his childhood and substituting artificial flowers for fresh ones in all the vases because then they would never need changing. The ladies persevered so successfully, however, that he soon gave up taking lunch out and deigned to share one precise hour of conversation with them each evening prior to retiring promptly at ten. Spencer's toleration even extended to providing temporary accommodation for Beatrice Potter (the future Beatrice Webb) in

1891, when she was working on Charles Booth's great survey of poverty in London. When she went so far as to invite trade unionist informants round for dinner even she felt that the gesture amounted almost to *lèse-majesté*, as she noted in a letter to her future husband, Sidney Webb: "To think that his august drawing-room is nightly the scene of socialistic talk, clouds of tobacco, aided with whisky."

Spencer also enjoyed the company of George Eliot whom he curiously complimented as "the most admirable woman, mentally, I have ever met".   They met for the first time in 1851 and, before she switched her affections to G.H. Lewes, to whom Spencer himself had introduced her, the attraction seems to have been much stronger on her side than on his; at any rate he appears to have gone to some pains after her death to dispel any rumour that they might ever have been more than friends.

Even more valued was the companionship of his near neighbour T. H. Huxley, a friend for over thirty years, "who routinely subjected the poly-math's wilder flights of generalisation to cool scrutiny."   Spencer was nevertheless acknowl-edged by contemporaries as one of the intellectual giants of his century, to rank beside Carlyle and ahead of Ruskin. His works were read and re-spected as far away as Japan. His legacy has proved less durable than his reputation. The dis-tinguished social scientist Stanislav Andreski has asserted that "Spencer is not regarded as impor-tant by the historians of biology ... *The Principles of Psychology* had little influence on the develop-ment of its subject" . In sociology and anthropol-ogy his evolutionist perspective, however, proved more valuable, especially in regard to such topics as the process of state formation. Andreski like-wise notes that of Spencer that "though widely applauded, his eloquent tirades against govern-mental regulation had little relevance to the ills of the Victorian Britain which was the most unbureaucratic large-scale society which ever existed". John Stuart Mill perhaps best summa-rised the inherent limitations of Spencer's hubristic intellect when he observed that he was "so good that he ought to be better".

T.H. HUXLEY

T.H. Huxley (1825-1895) invented the term 'biol-ogy ' and devoted his life to establishing it as an academic discipline. Graduating from Charing Cross Hospital, like Darwin he circumnavigated the world, serving as assistant surgeon aboard *HMS Rattlesnake*. The voyage involved a sojourn in Australia, where he met his future wife, Anne

82. *Thomas Henry Huxley.*

83. *Huxley's house in North Bank.*

Heathorn, and also enabled him to collect data on jellyfish which, when published as a scientific paper, won him election as a Fellow of the Royal Society at the astonishingly early age of 26. By then he was living in the house of his brother George at 41 North Bank (demolished *c.*1890). Searching for "some place with a decent address, cheap and beyond all things clean", he subsequently tried St Anne's Gardens, 1 Edward Street and 4 Upper York Place. Having left the Navy but lacking secure employment, Huxley persevered with part time lecturing and writing, convinced that "my course in life is taken. I will not leave London – I will make myself a name and position as well as an income by some kind of pursuit connected with science, which is the thing Nature fitted me for if she fitted me for anything".

In 1854 Huxley became lecturer in Natural History at the Royal School of Mines at £200 a year and soon proved himself a superb teacher, capable of lecturing to "hard-headed fellows who live among facts" as effectively as to specialist audiences. In 1855 he was appointed consultant naturalist to the Geological Survey and was therefore at last financially steady enough to marry Anne Heathorn, after an engagement of seven years. Prior to the wedding, Anne was installed in lodgings at 8 Titchfield Terrace. Her health had

been so drained by the long voyage from Australia that a specialist gave her only six months to live. Huxley's response was "six months or not, she is going to be my wife !" Darwin, already a good friend, wrote half-mockingly "I hope your marriage will not make you idle: happiness I fear is not good for work". It was a superfluous injunction to a man who lived to work. And, although Anne often complained that Huxley too often did put his work first, visitors to their home invariably remarked on its atmosphere of domestic contentment.

In 1859 Darwin published his epochal *Origin of Species.* and Huxley, in effect, reviewed it warmly for *The Times.* The book had in fact been sent to a journalist called Lucas, who lived in Alexandra Road and confessed himself utterly ignorant of science. A friend suggested enlisting the aid of Huxley, then living at 14 Waverley Place. The review, three and a half columns long, was prefaced by a couple of introductory paragraphs by Lucas and appeared over his name. But the analysis, and enthusiasm, were pure Huxley.

Personally sceptical in matters of religion (and royalty), Huxley thought his parents had been unwittingly prescient in naming him Thomas. He described his own theological position in another word he coined himself – agnostic'. Biblical fundamentalism outraged him: "Whenever we try to march towards the truth, we find our way blocked by Noah and his Ark". But, though a zealot for experiment and system, he was wary of simple-minded positivism and of the process of scientific discovery itself once observed that "it is the customary fate of new truths to begin as heresies and to end as superstitions".

In 1861 Huxley's first-born, blond, blue-eyed

84. *The Presbyterian church in Marlborough Place, a familiar landmark during Huxley's residence in this street.*

Noel, died suddenly of scarlet fever at the age of four. His memory made Waverley Place unbearable and the Huxleys moved to 26 Abercorn Place. Huxley described their new residence in a note to Spencer – "beyond the facts that we have a lunatic neighbour on one side, and an empty house on the other, that it has cost me twice as much to get into my house as I expected, that the cistern began to leak and spoil the ceiling and other such small drawbacks, the new house is a decided success."

In 1872 Huxley moved his much expanded family to 4 Marlborough Place, where he enlarged an existing white-painted, deep-eaved cottage by adding a large extension built in yellow brick, with very large windows. Huxley's son wrote affectionately, and with disarming understatement, that the resulting edifice "was not without character, and certainly was unlike most London houses. It was built for comfort, not beauty; designed, within stringent limits as to cost, to give each member of the family room to get away by himself or herself if so disposed". The house was also large enough to have guests stay over and to enable the

family to entertain all-comers on Sunday evenings, offering "a cold supper with varying possibilities in the direction of dinner or tea." The normal entertainment was home-made music but on one celebrated occasion Sir Henry Irving was present "and recited *'Eugene Aram'* with great effect". The conversation was wide-ranging, often speculative "yet kept within such bounds that bishop or archbishop might have listened without offence". Spencer, a frequent visitor, sent a new clock as a house-warming present – "to express in some way more emphatic than by words, my sense of the many kindnesses I have received at your hand", adding as a joke that it might make up for all the 'time' Huxley had spent in careful criticism of his writings.

John Fiske, who attended one of Huxley's Sunday evening 'tall teas', thought the house was "the nearest to an earthly paradise of anything that I have seen", occupied by "seven of the loveliest children that ever live". After retreating for a smoke in Huxley's study – "the cosiest I have seen in England"– Fiske left his "warm-hearted and lovable" hosts with their injunction that there would be a plate set for me every Sunday " ringing in his ears.

Scholarly productivity in no way distracted Huxley from onerous administrative duties. Between 1862 and 1884 he served on no less than ten royal commissions and was secretary to the Royal Society from 1871 to 1880 and its president from 1883 to 1885. From 1870 to 1872 he was also a member of the newly established London School Board and exerted a decisive influence on the shaping of the curriculum of the first state schools. No early riser, Huxley habitually worked far into the night and eventually undermined his own health by his own efforts. Illness plagued him increasingly from 1885 and in 1890 he retired from St John's Wood to live by the sea at Eastbourne, where he died.

BRADLAUGH, BESANT AND BLAVATSKY

The views of freethinker **Charles Bradlaugh** (1833-1891) were once summarised by an Archbishop of York as "No God, no king and as few people as possible." Unlike Spencer, Bradlaugh believed that the intellectual should be committed to an active role in society rather than serving as its detached observer. A trained lawyer and, more to the point, a powerfully built man, Bradlaugh first achieved national notoriety in 1866 when, during riots over threatened restrictions on Sunday trading, he led the mob which pulled down the railings around Hyde Park. It was this incident which led the authorities to concede a customary

85. *Charles Bradlaugh.*

86. *Charles Bradlaugh's library in Circus Road.*

right of free expression at what became known as Speaker's Corner. Bradlaugh himself would have made an ideal 'regular' there; his booming voice once enabled him to address a rally of 30,000 gathered in Trafalgar Square.

In that same turbulent year of 1866 Bradlaugh established the National Secular Society to agitate for mass education, land reform, republicanism and self-government for India. In 1880, as newly elected MP for Northampton, he hit the headlines again when he refused to swear the oath of allegiance on the Bible, demanding the right, as an atheist, simply to affirm. Banned from taking his seat in consequence, he was repeatedly re-elected by the stubborn burghers of Northampton until 1886 when a change in the occupancy of the office of Speaker of the House of Commons allowed for a revision of the time-honoured convention, confirmed by a statute which Bradlaugh himself promoted. In parallel with this Bradlaugh, who moved into 10 Circus Road in 1879, found another way of outraging Victorian sensibilities by distributing an American publication on birth-control, somewhat opaquely entitled *Fruits of Philosophy*. His partner in this enterprise was **Annie Besant**

87. Circus Road, c.1906.

(1847-1933), a Londoner of Irish descent, who had married a clergyman and, discovering his proclivity for wife-battering, left him. Petite and bright-eyed, Besant had met Bradlaugh through the National Secular Society, whose campaigning activities uncovered her considerable talents as a platform speaker in the cause of atheism. In due course she would discover many other causes.

A prosecution arising from the 'physiological pamphlet' might have ruined Bradlaugh had not one Henry Turberville, the eccentric brother of the novelist R.D. Blackmore, quixotically decided to leave Bradlaugh the bulk of his property. But just before his death Turberville decided to change his bequest in favour of the pretty daughter of the chemist who provided his medicines. Blackmore, enraged by this, joined forces with Bradlaugh to contest the matter and a compromise left Bradlaugh better off to the tune of £2,500. It was this victory which enabled Bradlaugh and his daughters, 'with one little servant much given to fainting', to move into 10 Circus Road, where they occupied the top floor and the basement, the ground floor and first floor being let to a firm of music-sellers. Books overflowed everywhere – 6,000 volumes and 3,000 government Blue Books. They were the household's only luxury, rumours to the contrary not-

withstanding. The furniture was sparse and simple and Bradlaugh was indifferent to food, except in regard to the punctuality of its production. When he died, insolvent, his creditors agreed to accept ten shillings in the pound as his library was broken up and sold by mail order.

The colourful life of **Madame Blavatsky** (1831-1891) was to become indirectly intertwined with that of Bradlaugh through their common connection with Annie Besant. Born in Russia of German aristocratic descent, Helena Paulovna Hahn at seventeen married a Russian officer, Nicephore Blavatsky, but soon separated from him to travel, notably, she claimed in India and Tibet. In 1873 she pitched up in the USA and in 1875 co-founded the Theosophical Society to promote a syncretistic faith, derived partly from her own eclectic interpretation of Brahmin and Buddhist scriptures, and buttressed by unacknowledged gleanings from standard works on Freemasonry, Gnosticism and Spiritualism. In 1877 she published Isis Unveiled and in 1879, as if to add an extra authenticity to her standing as a guru, established a branch of the Theosophical Society in Bombay. The world headquarters of the movement was located, however, at 19 Avenue Road, St John's Wood. Despite an unprepossessing appearance – "globular in

89. Annie Besant.

88. The Reformers' Memorial at Kensal Green Cemetery. It features St John's Wood residents Herbert Spencer and Charles Bradlaugh.

shape, with a dull grey complexion, a far from attractive physiognomy and eyes like discoloured turquoises" – she attracted thousands of followers, though the Irish poet W.B. Yeats rather disconcertingly described her as being "a sort of female Dr Johnson". In 1884 Blavatsky's claims to mystic powers were unequivocally denounced by the Society for Psychical Research as unabashed charlatanry and she found it suddenly convenient to retire to Italy. In 1888 she published another scriptural volume, *The Secret Doctrine*. At the time of her death she was estimated to have 100,000 followers worldwide. In Annie Besant, moreover, she had recruited a disciple who would outshine the prophet.

In 1885 **Annie Besant** had joined the Fabian Society and become for a while an ardent socialist, getting caught up in the 'Bloody Sunday' Trafalgar Square riot of 1887 and playing a leading part in the landmark strike of 1888 organised by the girls at Bryant and May's match factory in the East End. Drifting out of Bradlaugh's sphere, she resisted George Bernard Shaw's proposal that she should co-habit with him and instead became a fervent convert to theosophy. Visiting India in 1893, Besant convinced herself that India, and not England, was the true land of her birth and undertook a serious study of Hindu philosophy, publishing works on religion which were far more creditable than those of her mentor. As well as promoting theosophy, she became passionately involved in the movement for Indian independence. Backed by the Maharajah of Benares, she established a college and a girls' school which became the nucleus of a full-blown Hindu university. From 1907 until her death she served as President of the Theosophical Society, though her claim that her adopted Madrasi son, Krishnamurti, was the Messiah tested the allegiance of many of the faithful. In 1918 her devotion to the independence struggle won extraordinary recognition in her election as President of the Indian National Congress, the first woman or westerner ever to hold such exalted office. Her opposition to violence, however, soon sidelined her in the nationalist movement, although she did succeed in winning support for it among British Labour politicians. At her death she was cremated on an Indian seashore.

FOUNDER OF GIRTON

Another St John's Wood resident who faced tough opposition for her convictions was the suffragette, **Emily Davies** (1830-1921). Her clergyman father gave her a fervent Evangelical upbringing but little formal education. This latter deficiency shaped the rest of her life. At the age of 24 she met Elizabeth Garrett and became an enthusiastic supporter of her efforts to enter the medical profession but swiftly abandoned any similar ambitions for herself, largely for lack of the requisite qualifications. Following the death of her father in 1861 Emily Davies was able to move to London where she was soon contributing to the first British feminist publication *The English Woman's Journal*. In 1862 her article on Female Physicians argued that many women would *prefer* to consult a doctor of their own sex and that if female physicians focused on the diseases of women and children they would have a quite sufficient field of action without invading the male sphere.

Having narrowly failed to persuade the progressive, non-denominational University of London to admit women as students, Davies, as honorary secretary of the Kensington Society, a feminist discussion group, became deeply involved in 1866 in presenting the first petition to Parliament requesting votes for women. Philosopher and Liberal MP John Stuart Mill (1806-1873) advised the group, which included his wife Harriet Taylor, on the wording of their petition and undertook himself to present it to the Commons.

Davies's personal instinct was for a non-confrontational strategy and she directly criticised colleagues such as Barbara Bodichon for their more shrill approach. She was also convinced that association with 'wild people' could only damage reformist causes in a deeply conservative society like England and was therefore not above stage-managing public meetings by packing the front rows with the prettiest and meekest-looking females she could find.

In the same year as the suffrage petition was presented Davies published *The Higher Education of Women*. Her major argument was that as it was generally agreed that it was beneficial that females should have some form of elementary education it was illogical not to allow them to proceed as far as their abilities could carry them.

Following the failure of the suffrage petition to achieve female enfranchisement as part of the Second Reform Act of 1867, Davies distanced herself from the agitation for the vote to concentrate on establishing a college of higher education for women. What became Girton College, Cambridge opened at Hitchin, Hertfordshire in 1869 with just six students. It transferred to the uni-

90. Emily Davies.

versity city in 1873. In its early days Girton was an austere institution. Davies refused to spend money on landscaping the grounds and could not afford to supply her students' rooms with more than the barest essentials. Such poverty proved a blessing in disguise as the girls enthusiastically plundered second-hand shops and improvised their own decorations to give each room an individual rather than an institutional look. It proved, by default, to be a most liberating experience. Davies herself seems to have assumed that her girls should be always at their books and concerned herself little with the need to develop the college as a community. Perhaps she was correct in believing that this would take care of itself.

As for those parents who were fearful that a college education would seduce their daughters from the path of domestic bliss, Davies bade them consider the alternatives that beckoned to a strong-willed and intellectually adventurous girl – traipsing round the slums with housing reformer Octavia Hill or, worse still, slopping out hospital wards under the supervision of Miss Nightingale.

Once Girton was firmly established Emily Davies returned to London and became committed to the women's suffrage movement again. In 1919 she became one of the few survivors of the original petitioning group of 1866 actually to cast a vote as a woman, following the passage of the Representation of the People Act in 1918. A blue plaque marks her home at 17 Cunningham Place.

TWENTIETH CENTURY NOTABLES

At 103 Hamilton Terrace lived **Joseph Herman Hertz** (1872-1946). Born in Slovakia, but educated in the United States since he was 14, he was despatched as a novice rabbi to Johannesburg in 1898. Having been temporarily expelled from the Transvaal for his outspoken criticism of religious bigotry, he subsequently became Professor of Philosophy at Transvaal University College. In 1913 he was appointed Chief Rabbi of the United Hebrew Congregations of the British Empire and in this post he displayed what the *Dictionary of National Biography* records as "an explosive energy which almost scandalized the conservative elements of his flock". Hertz vigorously denounced Russian persecutions of Jews, conducted a vigorous campaign against the emerging movement of Liberal Jewry and passionately endorsed the 1917 Balfour Declaration which committed the British government to support the establishment of a Jewish homeland in Palestine.

Much of the inter-war period he devoted to warning the public of the danger posed by Nazism and the consequent need for safe havens for Jewish refugees. There was a Churchillian quality to both his appearance and his character. Stocky and egotistical, Hertz embodied a quixotic combination of courage and compassion, bellicosity and kindliness.

Psychologist **Melanie Klein** (1882-1960) was born in Vienna and trained as an analyst in Budapest and Berlin. Her major preoccupation was the application of psychoanalysis to children. A blue plaque records her residence at 42 Clifton Hill.

The intellectual ambitions of **Arnold Toynbee** (1889-1975) were only slightly less monumental than those of Herbert Spencer. He confined himself to history – pretty well all of it. During much of the interwar period Toynbee lived at 3 Melina Place. Originally a specialist on Byzantium, he also worked as a political analyst for the Foreign Office in both world wars, as well as serving as director of the Royal Institute of International Affairs from 1925 to 1955. His *magnum opus*, modestly entitled *A Study of History*, was published in twelve volumes between 1934 and 1961. Comparing the rise and fall of over two dozen major civilizations, Toynbee argued that the history of mankind should be essentially interpreted as a process of response to challenges. British academics, particularly historians, have never had much regard for system-builders, but even *The Cambridge Guide to English Literature* concedes that many scholars regard the *Study* "as the finest work by a historian since Gibbon's *Decline and Fall*."

Travers Christmas Humphreys (1901-1983) had

91. Arnold Toynbee.

a brilliant legal career which, in the opinion of colleagues, could have been even more brilliant if he had been more interested in the law and less interested in Buddhism. He certainly came from the right background, being the son of Sir Richard Humphreys (1867-1956), a master of the criminal law, who was a member of the legal teams which secured convictions in such celebrated cases as those of Oscar Wilde, Dr Crippen, 'Brides in the Bath' murderer G.J. Smith, Sir Roger Casement and Horatio Bottomley. A convert to Buddhism while still a schoolboy, Christmas Humphreys founded the London Buddhist Lodge – later the Buddhist Society – in 1924, becoming its first president, an office which he was to retain for half a century. His many publications about his adopted faith included one lucid exposition which sold half a million copies. He also wrote passable poetry. Another of this eminent counsel's firm convictions was that the true author of Shakespeare's plays and poems was the Earl of Oxford and in support of this belief he served as President of the Shakespearian Authorship Society. Interestingly for someone of his adopted faith Humphreys played a leading role in the war-crimes trials in Japan. He also served as a High Court judge from 1950 to 1959. As a judge he was frequently criticised for leniency – perhaps a permissible failing in a Buddhist. He died at his home, 58 Marlborough Place, where Buddhist meetings had been held for many years and which, childless, he bequeathed to the Zen Trust.

Living off Letters

Writing in 1852 American journalist and travel writer Henry Tuckerman offered his readers the intriguing proposition that there might be a causal relationship between English suburban comfort and literary productivity:

> "The feel of a carpet, the support of an arm-chair and the sight of curtains and a fire possess charms unknown where a gay street population and gardens under a bright sky make it a sacrifice to remain in the house ... Where there is isolation, comfort is studied; domesticity engenders mental occupation; and hence the prolific authorship of the British metropolis ... The reserve and individuality of English life, surrounded but never invaded by the multitude, gives singular intensity to reflection ... the spectacle of concentrated human life, and its daily panorama, incites the creative powers ...."

Tuckerman's Law certainly holds good north of Regent's Park.

IN THRALL TO THE MUSE

In the nineteenth century the poet stood higher, perhaps, in public esteem than any other type of creative artist; and among their ranks probably only Tennyson himself stood higher than **Robert Browning** (1812-1889). A Browning Society was established in the poet's honour in 1881, while he was still alive. Following the death of his wife, the poet Elizabeth Barrett, in 1861 Browning had left Italy, where they had lived throughout their fifteen-year marriage, and settled at 19 Delamere Terrace, which was to be his home until 1887. It was there that he composed one of his most successful works *The Ring and the Book* (1868-9).

Sir Lewis Morris (1833-1907), who lived at 42 Randolph Avenue, wrote much poetry in the style of Tennyson, but not nearly as well. When he complained that lack of critical appreciation of his work implied a conspiracy of silence against him Oscar Wilde opined that if such a conspiracy *did* exist he should join it. Morris was nevertheless astounded not to be offered the Laureateship following Tennyson's death. Welsh as it were by conviction as well as by birth, Morris chaired the organising committee of the National Eisteddfod for over twenty years, campaigned vigorously for Welsh Home Rule and also played a leading role in the establishment of the University of Wales, serving as its first chancellor.

German-born **Mathilde Blind** (1841-1896) came to England as a child, the step-daughter of a refugee

92. Robert Browning.

from the failed revolutions of 1848, and grew up at 28 Townshend Road. She therefore had an entirely English education but still wrote fluently in German. Her compositions ranged from a polemical poem against Highland evictions to a play about Robespierre and the first biography of George Eliot. Her most important work *The Ascent of Man* (1888) was inspired by Darwin's theory of evolution. One critic gave it the curiously back-handed compliment of being "fine only in parts but the finest parts are very fine". Her friend and fellow-countryman Ludwig Mond paid for it to be re-issued after her death and raised a monument to her memory. The last years of her life were passed at 1 St. Edmund's Terrace, Ford Madox Brown's old house.

Francis Thompson (1859-1907), having withdrawn from his first vocation, the priesthood, and failed to qualify as a doctor (after six years of study) drifted from his native Lancashire to London, where he was soon reduced to selling matches and sleeping on the streets. Rescued by the publisher Wilfred Meynell and his wife Alice, who took him into their home for years at a time and repeatedly paid for monastic retreats which gave periods of stability to his life, Thompson struggled unsuccessfully to break an addiction to opium,

93. John Masefield.

94. Mary Howitt.

which he had initially used as a pain-killer against the tuberculosis that eventually killed him. By the time he was finally taken into the Hospital of St John and St Elizabeth he weighed just seventy pounds. He is chiefly remembered for a religious poem *The Hell Hound*. Rossetti considered Thompson to be "the greatest poet of Catholicism since Dante".

Ernest Dowson (1867-1900) lived at 15 Bristol Gardens from 1889 to 1894, the year of his father's suicide, which impelled him into a nomadic existence, restlessly travelling between London, France and Ireland. A friend of Wilde and Aubrey Beardsley, Dowson contributed to the notorious *Yellow Book* and was both an habitué of the Cafe Royal and a member of the Rhymers' Club which met at Ye Olde Cheshire Cheese in Fleet Street. Although he wrote both romantic and devotional verse many of his poems exude a world-weariness which anticipated his early death. It is perhaps appropriate that Dowson's best-known line was "They are not long, the days of wine and roses".

The intended maritime career of **John Masefield** (1878-1967) was abruptly curtailed by acute seasickness, followed by desertion. After publishing poems, plays and short stories, Masefield finally came to public attention with a long narrative poem, *The Everlasting Mercy*, which he composed while living at 30 Maida Avenue. Colloquial, uninhibited and with just a whiff of blasphemy about it, the poem proved a sensation. Masefield went on to be popular, productive and successful

until fame finally did for him and he was appointed Poet Laureate in 1930.

Belfast-born **(Frederick) Louis MacNeice** (1907-1963) collected a first at Oxford, where he befriended Auden and Spender. In 1941 he abandoned an academic career to join the BBC as a writer-producer, gaining an outstanding reputation for documentaries and dramas, such as *Christopher Columbus* (1944), written while he was living at 10 Wellington Place. Apart from his own technically accomplished, quirky verse, MacNeice produced essays, plays, acclaimed translations of the *Agamemnon* of Aeschylus and Goethe's *Faust*, a book on Yeats and an unfinished volume of autobiography.

VERSATILE PENS

Cyrus Redding (1785-1870) was a tireless hack who first came to London from his native Cornwall at twenty-one, worked on provincial newspapers, served as a correspondent in Paris and produced a vast variety of works, ranging from guide books to a history of wine and studies of shipwrecks and misers. His friends included the painter Turner, the poet Thomas Campbell, the eccentric millionaire author William Beckford and the exiled salon hostess Madame de Stael. Redding lived in Hill Road and periodically wrote for another local resident, Douglas Jerrold.

William Howitt (1792-1879) and his wife **Mary** (1799-1888) lived from 1848 to 1852 at the then No. 28 Avenue Road, a failed newspaper venture having forced them to move out of their Surrey home and take a smaller house. William wrote travel books, while Mary was a novelist, translator and poet. Dickens solicited contributions from her for the early numbers of his own publication *Household Words*. She might therefore be slightly disappointed to know that her most lasting literary legacy was the children's rhyme 'Won't you walk into my parlour?, Said the spider to the fly'. Mary Howitt was also a member of the Kensington Society, the pioneering feminist group of which Emily Davies (*see* p.74) was secretary. The Howitts' St John's Wood residence became something of a *salon*, where their guests included founding members of the Pre-Raphaelite Brotherhood, such as Dante Rossetti and Holman Hunt, as well as the sculptor Thomas Woolner (newly returned from the Australian gold-fields), the novelist Mrs Gaskell and numerous refugee intellectuals.

John Gibson Lockhart (1794-1854) was the son-in-law of Sir Walter Scott, who thought him a handsome, charming, talented, excellent fellow and was rather bemused by his undoubted gift for making bitter enemies. Contemporaries thought Lockhart decidedly odd because he loathed hunting as a needless cruelty; but he did not extend his humanitarian tenderness to fellow authors. As a contributor to *Blackwood's Magazine*, Lockhart savaged Keats, Hazlitt, Leigh Hunt and other members of what he disdainfully dismissed as 'the Cockney school of poets'. Apart from editing the influential *Quarterly Review* for almost thirty years, Lockhart also wrote historical novels, translations from Spanish and German and biographies of Robert Burns and his father-in-law, the profits from the latter being turned over to Scott's creditors, a true act of literary *noblesse oblige*. Lockhart lived at 44 Abbey Road.

James Payn (1830-1898) was a regular contributor to Dickens' *Household Words* and edited *Chambers' Journal* (1859-74) and then the *Cornhill Magazine* (1882-96). During the latter period he lived at 43 Warrington Crescent. A fertile author of essays and memoirs, he also churned out over a hundred novels.

MR PUNCH'S PEOPLE

"I have now come to live in St John's Wood, and will therefore, like my great outlaw ancestor, henceforward be known as Hood of the Wood."

95. Warrington Crescent, home of James Payn.

This from the man who chided himself that he had to be "a lively Hood to get a livelihood". Little wonder that Mark Lemon, first editor of *Punch*, called **Thomas Hood** (1799-1845) the Professor of Punmanship. Hood and his family, after years of penury, moved into 17 Elm Tree Road in 1841, elated by the prospect of a secure £300 a year for editing the *New Monthly Magazine*, one of the many new publications, like *Punch* and the *Illustrated London News*, founded as a result of reductions in the "taxes on knowledge" brought about by the Liberal reformers of the 1830s. Hood's health, however, remained wretched; he was consumptive and suffered periodic bouts of rheumatic fever. But his spirits seem never to have dimmed and he was much loved as a father, friend, husband and host. He was particularly close to Douglas Jerrold, a fellow contributor to *Punch*. Dickens, Thackeray and the painter Daniel Maclise were among his admirers.

By New Year 1844 the Hood family had removed, for the first time in eight years, to a house of their own – Devonshire Lodge, (28) Finchley Road, "just beyond the Eyre Arms, three doors short of the turnpike". At the same time Hood, having parted company with the *New Monthly*, launched *Hood's Own*. Dickens and Browning helped with contributions. But by October Jane Hood was writing to an old friend that: "We fear the clay soil of this neighbourhood does not agree with him, and that we must move again, which we are sorry for, as we have a very pretty house. I am sorry to say he is never well now – unable to walk the shortest distance without suffering and feeling every change of weather." Hood knew that his end was approaching. So did his friends. Prime Minister Sir Robert Peel arranged a Civil List Pension of £100 a year for life for Mrs Hood. Hood, gallantly plying his pen almost to the last, died in May 1845, as he had himself predicted 'like a horse in harness'. A public subscription raised £1386 15s 6d for the benefit of his family. Contributions came from as far away as America where the poet Longfellow remembered "the pale face of the poet and the house in St. John's Wood" where he had once been entertained.

By the time **Douglas Jerrold** (1803-1857) became a successful dramatist at just fifteen years of age he had already been an actor, a sailor and a printer. Although Jerrold continued to churn out plays for the following twenty years, he turned increasingly to journalism and then to editing. A leading contributor to *Punch* from its beginning, he ended his career as editor of *Lloyd's Illustrated Weekly Newspaper*. He was a close friend of Dickens and Thackeray.

96. Thomas Hood.

Shirley Brooks (1816 -1874), who was editor of *Punch* from 1870 until his death, lived at 6 Kent Terrace and here, on one occasion, hosted a dinner-party at which the guests included Charles Kingsley, author of *The Water Babies*, Mark Twain and the painter W.P. Frith.

Joseph Hatton (1841-1907) wrote a memoir of the first editor of *Punch*, Mark Lemon, and, in a series of magazine articles, also sketched the publication's history. His own works included chronicling Henry Irving's *Impressions of America* and recording the *Reminiscences of J.L. Toole* (*see* p.116). Hatton lived successively at 9 Titchfield Terrace, 1 Grove End Road and 11 Marlborough Road. His daughter Bessie became a novelist.

Hatton's contemporary, **Clement William Scott** (1841-1904) contributed sentimental verse to *Punch* but was better known as the savage drama critic of the *Daily Telegraph* (1871-98) and editor of *The Theatre*. A friend of the younger Thomas Hood and of W.S. Gilbert, he was also the brother-in-law of George Du Maurier and claimed to have played in the first ever game of tennis, alongside its inventor, Major Wingfield. He was also an assiduous adapter of French plays for Squire Bancroft (*see* p. 117). Scott lived at 44 Clifton Road (East).

97. *Thomas Hood's house in Elm Tree Road, later the home of the St John's Wood Art Club.*

98. Douglas Jerrold.

99. J.L. Garvin.

THE JOURNALISTS

William Blanchard Jerrold (1826-1884), eldest son of Douglas Jerrold, followed his father into journalism, becoming the Paris correspondent of several English newspapers. He was a confidant of Napoleon III, a close friend of the artist Gustave Doré and a cultivated gourmet. On the death of his father he took over the editorship of *Lloyd's*. In 1872 Jerrold supplied the text for Doré's nightmarish book of engravings published under the title *London: A Vision* and later wrote a biography of the artist. He lived at 6 Warwick Avenue.

In 1897 **Clement King Shorter** (1857-1926) was editing five newspapers simultaneously. He went on to found both the *Sphere* and the *Tatler* and also wrote substantial studies of the Brontes, Napoleon, George Borrow and Samuel Johnson. Shorter lived at 16 Marlborough Place.

As editor of *The Observer* (1908-42) **J. L. Garvin** (1868-1947) made it financially sound and politically influential, as well as creating an entirely new type of Sunday newspaper which combined serious analysis with extensive coverage of the arts. Garvin overcame an impoverished background and patchy education (he taught himself French, German and Spanish) to become not only one of the giants of Fleet Street but also editor of the 13th and 14th editions of the *Encyclopaedia Britannica*. A dazzling conversationalist and gifted with an elephantine memory, Garvin also found time to write a hefty three volume biography of Joseph Chamberlain.

PART-TIME PRODUCTIVITY

While most nineteenth century writers cobbled together an income by writing whatever they could be paid for, some followed a regular career, writing in their off-duty hours. The latter included **William Michael Rossetti** (1829-1919), son of a former revolutionary and Professor of Italian at King's College, London. He served in the Excise Office, ancestor of the Inland Revenue, from 1845 until 1894, where he used his expert knowledge of art to appraise paintings offered in lieu of estate duty. From 1850 he was art critic of the *Spectator* and contributed articles on art to the *Encyclopaedia Britannica*. In his youth Rossetti edited *The Germ*, the journal of the Pre-Raphaelite Brotherhood, himself composing the verses which adorned its cover. But he soon detached himself, intellectually

100. William Michael Rossetti.

101. Richard Garnett.

at least, from his elder brother Dante Gabriel Rossetti (1828-1882) and his circle of adoring acolytes, though there was no personal breach and at one point he did share a Cheyne Walk house with both Dante and the poet Swinburne. William Rossetti's true métier was poetry. He wrote biographies of Shelley and Keats, produced editions of Coleridge, Milton and Blake and introduced the work of Walt Whitman to British readers. With fraternal piety he devoted much of his later years to editing the collected works of his brother Dante and sister, the poet Christina Rossetti (1830-1894). In 1874 Rossetti married Emma Lucy, the daughter of Ford Madox Brown. He died at 3 St. Edmund's Terrace, next door to the former home of his father-in-law.

Despite a rather limited formal education **Richard Garnett** (1835-1906) soon proved himself a gifted linguist, following his father into the service of the British Museum and attracting the attention of the visionary librarian of the British Museum, Sir Anthony Panizzi (1797-1879). Garnett rose to become superintendent of the Reading Room (1875-90), then devoted himself to the Herculean task of supervising the completion of the printed Catalogue of its holdings. Almost a caricature of the shy, scholarly librarian, Garnett was renowned for his intellectual generosity. Subsisting plainly on a diet of sausage and mash, Garnett in his leisure hours wrote numerous biographies, poetry and a history of Italian Literature. Garnett lived

at 4 St. Edmund's Terrace and was a close friend of **Edmund Gosse** (1849-1928) who was described by H.G. Wells as "the official British man of letters". Gosse lived for over twenty years at 29 Delamere Terrace, which became a familiar port of call for such luminaries as Browning, Swinburne and Henry James. The autobiographical *Father and Son* (1907) was acknowledged as Gosse's masterpiece, an acutely observed evocation of his Devon childhood under the tyrannical regime of a parent who was both an eminent zoologist and a relentless member of the Plymouth Brethren. Gosse escaped to work first of all in the British Museum and then as a translator for the Board of Trade. He knew the Pre-Raphaelites, wrote biographies of Donne, Congreve and Gray and was instrumental in introducing the works of Ibsen and Gide to English audiences.

Leon Paul Blouet (1848-1903) graduated to full-time writing just short of his fortieth year. Having fought as a cavalry officer in the Franco-Prussian war (1870-71) and been severely wounded, he emigrated to England and became a teacher of French at St Paul's School (1876-87). As 'Max O' Rell', Blouet became a humorous commentator on Anglo-Saxon culture and customs on both sides of the Atlantic, producing both articles and books, which disarmed with such flattery and affection that he could tell home truths with double effect when he wished to. The epitome of the witty and charming Frenchman, he was much in demand as

102. Edmund Gosse.

103. Katherine Mansfield.

a speaker. A light-hearted treatment of the national mourning which accompanied the death of Queen Victoria proved, however, so ill-judged that it virtually destroyed his eminence at a stroke and he felt obliged to vacate his Acacia Road home and move to Paris, where he died soon afterwards.

W.W. Jacobs (1863-1943), the son of a Wapping wharfinger, managed to become a civil service clerk. The success of his short stories, which typically focused on shore-leave sailors, country characters or the macabre, eventually enabled him to become a full-time writer. He moved to Elm Tree Mansions in 1937 and subsequently died there.

TOUCHED BY TRAGEDY

John Davidson (1857-1909) was a prickly Scotsman who was free in his criticisms of others but never quite fulfilled his own promise. A son of the manse and a reluctant schoolmaster ("Nine - tenths of my time has been wasted in endeavouring to earn a livelihood"), he came to London in desperation, having already published poetry, a novel and two plays. He settled at 19 Warrington Crescent, where he lived from 1889 to 1909. A fringe member of the Rhymers' Club and a friend of Gosse, Davidson used a cash gift from George Bernard Shaw, which was intended to enable him to concentrate on his poetry, to write an historical

melodrama instead. Despairing of its acceptance and fearing the onset of cancer, Davidson drowned himself off the coast of Cornwall.

New Zealand-born **Katherine Mansfield** (1888-1923) was arguably the century's finest writer of short stories. In 1908-9 she was a music student at Beauchamp Lodge, 2 Warwick Crescent. After a brief disastrous marriage, in 1911 she met John Middleton Murry (1889-1957), whom she was eventually to marry in 1918. In 1915 they were living at 5 Acacia Road. Katherine's brother came to visit them there while he was on leave from the army, but a few days later he was killed in action in France. The memory of his happy visit became so unbearable to her that they left the house shortly afterwards. Katherine herself died of TB at thirty-five.

...BUT NOT LEAST

Humorist **Stephen Potter** (1900-1969) was an editor and radio producer, but is best known as the author of *"The Theory and Practice of Gamesmanship; or the Art of Winning Games without Actually Cheating"*. The book added a word to the English language and enjoyed cult status following its publication in 1947. In the 1960s Potter lived at 23 Maida Vale and at 23 Hamilton Terrace and played a leading role in conservation efforts to preserve the character of St John's Wood in the face of threats of inappropriate development.

The Novelists

With the very notable exception of George Eliot most of the novelists who have lived in St John's Wood have been rather minor stars in the great constellation of English literature.

Irish-born **Captain (Thomas) Mayne Reid** (1818-1883) emigrated to America in 1840, enlisted in the army, fought gallantly in the Mexican war (1846-48) and was seriously wounded at the storming of Chapultepec. Afterwards he travelled extensively and adventurously in the West, working variously as a storekeeper, actor, editor, trader and trapper. Returning to Europe, Reid drew on his real life experiences to write some ninety novels with rousing titles such as *The Rifle Rangers* and *The Scalp Hunters*. The more pacific side of his character was revealed in a handbook on croquet. Reid died at 12 Blomfield Road.

East-ender **Jerome K. Jerome** (1859-1927) started out as an actor before writing droll sketches based on his theatrical experiences. He found lasting fame with the cult classic *Three Men in a Boat* (1889), composed while he was living at 7 Alpha Place. Shortly afterwards he was turned out so that the Great Central Railway could build over the site of his home. Having claimed to have spent £450 on adapting it to his needs, Jerome was sufficiently disgusted with the compensation offered to him to take the railway company to court. Unfortunately the jury did not see things his way and he ended up in the decidedly unfunny position of being even worse off.

Maurice Hewlett (1861-1923), who lived at 7 Northwick Terrace, trained as a lawyer but had such success with his first novel, *The Forest Lovers*, a medieval romance, that he was able to devote himself full time to writing. His popularity was sustained until he turned to poetry.

Arthur Machen (1863-1947), son of a Welsh clergyman, came to London at seventeen. Employed to catalogue occult books, he joined the pseudo-mystical Order of the Golden Dawn whose other members included W.B. Yeats and Alisteir Crowley, "the wickedest man in the world". While living at 12 Melina Place Machen translated the memoirs of Casanova. He also worked as a Shakespearean actor and a journalist on the London *Evening News*, and eventually became renowned for supernatural tales of horror and evil.

Israel Zangwill (1864-1926) virtually created the Jewish genre novel single-handed with *Children of the Ghetto* (1892). His play *The Melting Pot* (1909) enjoyed huge success in the United States

104. *Jerome K. Jerome.*

105. *Israel Zangwill.*

and gave its title to the English language. Zangwill became a passionate Zionist in 1896 and devoted many years to the movement, though much of his effort proved fruitless.

Dorothy Richardson (1872-1957) lived at 32 Queen's Terrace in the summers of the years 1916-1938. Genteel poverty initially obliged her to survive as a governess, secretary, teacher, clerk, translator and journalist. Encouraged by H.G. Wells, she eventually embarked on a career as a novelist, pioneering the 'stream of consciousness' technique. Virginia Woolf credited her with inventing "the psychological sentence of the feminine gender". Angus Wilson hailed her achievement in revealing the struggles of an "utterly underprivileged woman in a world made by men for men". Feminist critics and publishers rediscovered her in the 1970s, when her autobiographical novel sequence *Pilgrimage* was reissued by Virago in four volumes.

Winifred Holtby (1898-1935) is best known for her last novel, *South Riding,* published the year after her early death, but her reputation was established while she was living in a mansion apartment in Maida Vale between 1923 and 1927,

106. Mansion flats in Maida Vale.

when she published *Anderby Wold* (1923), *The Crowded Street* (1924) and *The Land of Green Ginger* (1927). A vocal feminist and prolific journalist, she shared her home with Vera Brittain (1893-1970), who recorded the story of their relationship and Winifred's illness and death in *Testament of Friendship* (1940).

The earliest significant literary endeavours of **Nancy Mitford** (1904-1973) were volumes of family correspondence – *The Ladies of Alderley* (1938) and *The Stanleys of Alderley* (1939) – which were published while she was living at 13 Blomfield Road. Popular success came with her fourth novel *The Pursuit of Love* (1945). Her tales of reckless, feckless upper-class Bohemians won a wide readership but she is probably best remembered as the co-author of *Noblesse Oblige: an enquiry into the identifiable characteristics of the English aristocracy,* which introduced the notion of 'U' and 'non-U' to the English language.

PROPERTY AND PROPRIETY – THE SPHINX AT THE PRIORY

"We are, just as we were – thinking about the questionable house, and wondering what would be the right thing to do; hardly liking to lock up any money in land and bricks, and yet frightened lest we should not get a quiet place just where we want it."

Thus Mary Ann Evans – a.k.a. novelist ' George Eliot ' – writing to her constant correspondent Mrs Bray in June 1863. The 'questionable house' – The Priory, 21 North Bank – was finally taken a few

107. The drawing room of the Victorian novelist, Mrs Henry Wood, at 16 St John's Wood Park, c1887.

108. *Blomfield Road, home of Nancy Mitford.*

weeks later, "with the roses blooming all over it", for £2,000 on a 49-year lease.

Excluded from respectable circles by the irregular nature of her liaison with the journalist George Henry Lewes (1817-78) – who happened to have a wife and children elsewhere – George Eliot, holding herself to be married in the sight of a God she didn't believe in, compensated with property for what her domestic circumstances lacked in propriety. Successive literary triumphs, starting with *Adam Bede* (1859), brought rising financial rewards which supported a sequence of increasingly expensive establishments at ever more fashionable locations. The publication of *The Mill on the Floss* (1860) and *Silas Marner* (1861) opened the road from remote Richmond to St John's Wood – an undeniably fashionable address, but still not a particularly respectable one. As Lady Cork commented in a crushing aside – "Of course, poor dear, where else *could* she go? ".

The task of decorating The Priory was delegated to Owen Jones (1809-74), whose credentials could scarcely have been surpassed. As a young man Jones had studied at the Royal Academy and then travelled to remote Granada in Spain, where he made detailed drawings of the decor of the crumbling Alhambra palace, publishing the results of his labours as Britain's first colour-illustrated book. In 1851 Jones supervised the decoration of the Crystal Palace for the Great Exhibition and in 1856 published *The Grammar of Ornament*, a superb visual source-book which served as the prime reference tool for British art-schools for a generation. From the tenor of her recorded thoughts on the matter it is evident that the new mistress of

The Priory would have been relieved to have placed the responsibility for its refurbishment in hands far less expert – "thinking of carpets and tables is an affliction to me and seems like a nightmare from which I shall find it bliss to awake into my old world of care for things quite apart from upholstery."

After a purgatorial interlude during which their chosen abode was "all scaffolding and paint", the

109. *George Eliot.*

110. The drawing room at the Priory, home of George Eliot and G.H. Lewes.

Eliot-Lewes ménage took up occupation in November 1863. Two weeks later they were recorded as being "nearly in order, only wanting a few details of furniture to finish our equipment for a new stage in our life's journey." A house-warming was held on 24 November and by December the distaff side of the partnership could note with satisfaction that "we are enjoying ... the prettiness of colouring and arrangement, all of which we owe to our dear good friend Mr Owen Jones. He has determined every detail, so that we can have the pleasure of admiring what is our own without vanity."

A comfortable and undemanding daily routine was rapidly established – writing from nine until one, the afternoon being devoted to riding or walking in Regent's Park, the evening to reading or playing the piano. Occasionally there might be a visit to a concert or art gallery or the Zoo in the afternoon, or to the theatre in the evening. This orderly, reassuring framework was held precious, even inviolable – "to have a visitor stay with us would be a perturbation of our lives ... we cannot endure." It was, therefore, not until a couple of

years had passed that the partners began to entertain on a regular basis.

Even if their relationship had been regularised in the eyes of church, state and society, as a couple Eliot and Lewes struck contemporaries as improbable soul-mates, ill-matched for each other – except in point of plainness and a penchant for heavyweight German academic writing – and similarly ill-equipped for social success. Nicknamed 'the Sphinx' from her apparently aloof but omniscient manner, George Eliot was temperamentally incapable of flitting from subject to subject in conversation or person to person in social encounter. Once described as a woman who could talk "of Homer as simply as she would of flat-irons", the muse of North Bank was far more inclined to speak of the former than the latter. Lewes, fortunately, was a complementary opposite in personality. Variously described as resembling "an old-fashioned French barber or dancing-master" and an "unkempt Polish refugee", he was summarised as a personification of paradoxes, a scientist among literary men and a literary man among scientists, "a man of conscience wearing a mask

111. *George Henry Lewes.*

of flippancy", a "very ugly, very vivacious and very entertaining" character whose habitual dress "was an unlovely compromise between morning and evening costume, combining the less pleasing points of both." Lewes was adept at conversation, charades and introductions. While she sat by the fire, conversing intently with some favoured individual, he would circulate energetically, chaffing, cajoling and effervescing. Even so, hospitality was largely formalised into a Sunday afternoon ritual, underpinned by rules no less rigorous for being unwritten – women were not invited, but could ask to come; none of the author's books were to be so much as mentioned in passing; and guests were expected to leave promptly at six.

Despite these somewhat forbidding conventions regular visitors to The Priory included near neighbours Herbert Spencer and T.H. Huxley, Pre-Raphaelite artist Edward Burne-Jones, poets Robert Browning and Alfred Tennyson and Walter Bagehot, editor of *The Economist*. Other occasional callers included the redoubtable Dr Jowett of Balliol College, the painter Millais, the feminist campaigner Barbara Bodichon and the novelists Ivan Turgenev and Henry James, who described her as a 'horse-faced bluestocking' but found himself captivated by her nonetheless. But not even Lewes's best efforts and such galaxies of talent could guarantee a miracle of salon magic every week and on more than one occasion the gathering was rescued from outright dullness by the spritely

musical interventions of irrepressible George du Maurier, an accomplished performer of risqué French comic songs.

As early as the summer of 1864 George Eliot began to express concern for her partner's "delicate health". Horse-riding was attempted as a remedy but abandoned after a single trial as altogether too violent. Despite this anxiety, the novelist accounted them, at the end of their first year of residence, "happier than ever". Much of their mutual pleasure came simply from deep conversation.

In 1865 Lewes took up the heavy burden of the editorship of the new *Fortnightly*. In 1866 Eliot finished *Felix Holt*, receiving the princely sum of £5,000 from the publisher Blackwood for it. Between them they could now easily finance numerous trips abroad and to the country for the benefit of Lewes' failing health.

The first part of Eliot's masterpiece, *Middlemarch*, appeared in December 1871. Before the end of the decade it would earn her £8,000. The purchase of a carriage for £150 in 1873 might therefore be taken as a rather modest self-indulgence – though at that date such a sum would have furnished an entire three bedroom house or kept a country vicar and his household for a year.

Lewes finally died in December 1878 and with the passing of her 'dear companion' and 'greatest of blessings' George Eliot's tranquillity died also. For months she kept to the house, refusing visitors and leaving it only to be driven out beyond Kilburn, to open country where she could walk alone and unobserved. It seems possible that, in organising her former lover's papers to select items for posthumous publication, she discovered some proof of infidelity on his part. If this was the case it may serve to explain her otherwise seemingly capricious decision in May 1880 to marry Johnny Cross, her secretary, who was young enough to be her son. The event mystified as much as it scandalized many of her acquaintance. Abandoning St John's Wood, the newly-weds, after a lengthy Continental honeymoon, determined to settle in an imposing residence on exclusive Cheyne Walk in Chelsea but she was dead before the year was out.

Of The Priory, George Eliot's home for fifteen years, not a trace remains, North Bank having been swept away entirely by the building of the Great Central Railway extension in the 1890s. Ironically therefore it is the Cheyne Walk house, only fleetingly her dwelling, which bears the official LCC plaque honouring her memory. D.H. Lawrence neatly summarised George Eliot's literary achievement in a sentence: "it was she who started putting all the action inside".

In Harmony

MELODIOUS BEGINNINGS

St John's Wood's musical tradition dates back to its origins as a fashionable suburb. Despite his very un-Dutch name **Francois Joseph Dizi** (1780-?1840) was born in the Netherlands. He came to England at sixteen, determined to obtain instruction in the harp and for thirty years he was held to be the best harpist in the metropolis. He also owned a harp factory in Soho. In 1826 he was known to be living in Park Road, composing and teaching. He emigrated to Paris in 1830 and died there some time after 1840.

Neville Challoner (1784-?1835), after whom Neville Court is named, was living in Grove End Road in 1825. Trained as a violinist, Challoner worked as the band leader in the Richmond and Birmingham theatres and at Sadler's Wells before forming a music publishing partnership with Thomas Skillern in 1806. From 1809 to 1829 he was principal harpist at the Italian Opera and was also principal tenor for the Philharmonic Society. Challoner composed for harp, violin, piano and flute and had many private pupils in the St John's Wood area.

The career of **Maria Malibran** (1808-1836) began with a stage debut at the age of six. Driven by her demanding, domineering father, Manuel Garcia (1775-1832), who had built a career on promoting the works of Rossini outside that composer's native Italy, she went with the rest of her family to North America in 1825. They constituted, in effect, the first Italian opera company to cross the Atlantic. Malibran also made her London debut that same year in *The Barber of Seville*. An impetuous marriage to escape paternal tyranny swiftly failed and from 1828 to 1832 she sang alternately in London and Paris, then toured in Italy. Malibran made what was to be her last performance at Drury Lane. Having remarried and become pregnant she suffered a bad fall from her horse and died of the resulting gynaecological complications, just twenty-eight years of age. Marban Road may be a garbled tribute to her memory, it being difficult to imagine what connection it might otherwise have with a Bolivian province of that name.

Marietta Alboni (1826-1894), like Malibran, made a career out of the works of Rossini and was indeed coached by him personally. At his funeral she sang a duet with the great Adelina Patti. Alboni made her debut at sixteen and at twenty-one came to London to open the first season of the Royal Italian Opera at Covent Garden. After living in St John's Wood she eventually settled in Paris.

PRINCIPALS AND PRINCIPLES

Born the son of a dancing-master, **Sir George MacFarren** (1813-1887) helped to establish the Society of British Musicians when he was only 21 and was a Professor at the Royal Academy of Music by the time he was 24. At 32 he was appointed conductor at the Royal Opera House, Covent Garden. Thenceforth his brilliant prospects literally darkened as his eyesight progressively deteriorated. Total blindness forced him to abandon conducting in 1860 but he continued to teach, write, lecture and compose with undiminished determination, becoming both Professor of Music at Cambridge and Principal of the Royal Academy of Music. His symphonies and operas rarely met even moderate success but many of his numerous cantatas and oratorios became established favourites at provincial music festivals. His best known work today is the overture *Chevy Chase*. Knighted in 1883, this warm-hearted workaholic had, by the end of his remarkable career, become, in musical terms, a complete reactionary, resolutely opposed to virtually every significant new development in composition and performance and renowned as the epitome of the scholarly pedant. He lived initially at Marlborough Hill and then at 13 Blenheim Road.

Composer **Ferdinand Praeger** (1815-1891) was born in Leipzig, the son of an opera director. Initially trained to the cello, he switched to the piano at nine and was a noted teacher by the age of sixteen. At nineteen he moved to London, where he found many pupils. In 1842 he became the London correspondent of the *Neue Zeitung für Musik*. In the 1850s he hosted Wagner on his visit to London. Wagner judged Praeger to be "an unusually good-natured man, though one far too excitable for his standard of culture". Praeger subsequently exaggerated their intimacy at book length in *Wagner as I knew Him*. Its pretensions were later brutally exposed by Houston Stewart Chamberlain and the German edition was hastily withdrawn in 1893, shortly after Praeger's death.

As a very young child **Sir William Sterndale Bennett** (1816-1875) was a chorister at King's College, Cambridge. As a ten-year-old at the Royal Academy of Music he was sternly judged still more boy than musician but nevertheless achieved his first composition at twelve and sang in the choir at St Paul's Cathedral until his voice broke. An outstanding pianist, and, through this, an intimate friend of Mendelssohn from the age of sixteen, Bennett also conducted the first English performance of Bach's *St Matthew Passion* in 1854 and succeeded Wagner as conductor for the Philharmonic Society the following year. A year after that he was appointed Professor of Music at

Cambridge, where he astonished fellow dons by refusing to treat the post as a sinecure and introducing the novel notion that musicians should have to pass rigorous examinations, just like other students. Bennett's conscientiousness as an academic severely limited the time he could devote to composition and the death of his wife in 1862 proved a terrible and lasting deprivation. He nevertheless accepted the post of Principal of the Royal Academy of Music. Knighted in 1871, he moved in September 1873 to 66 St John's Wood Road, where he died. He was honoured with burial in Westminster Abbey. *The Dictionary of National Biography* noted with severe approval of his work that "he never wrote a bar of music that was commonplace".

THE COLONEL AND HIS CIRCLE

Self-styled 'Colonel' **James Henry Mapleson** (1830-1901) was to become one of the most influential impresarios in the history of opera, being responsible for the first London performances of *Abduction from the Seraglio, Carmen, The Damnation of Faust, Faust, The Force of Destiny, A Masked Ball, The Merry Wives of Windsor* and the complete *Ring* cycle. Having studied at the Royal Academy of Music and sung in Verona under the name Enrico Manriani, Mapleson took over the management of the Lyceum in 1861 and then of Her Majesty's Theatre the following year, staging Italian operas until Her Majesty's burned down in 1867. After an interval at Drury Lane, Mapleson re-opened a reconstructed Her Majesty's in 1877. In 1878 he crossed the Atlantic to take over the management of the Academy of Music in New York where, in the course of eight years, he presented nineteen different operas. He returned to England in 1886, took up residence at 62 Avenue Road, the house occupied and enlarged by the art dealer Gambart, and published *The Mapleson Memoirs* in 1888. Reviewing the *Memoirs* George Bernard Shaw opined that that they would prove "very amusing, especially to readers who, like the Colonel himself, have no suspicion that his record covers a period of hopeless decay".

Carolina Johanna Thèrese Tietjens (1831-1887) was one of Mapleson's most reliable discoveries. Born in Hamburg, she made her debut in the name role of Donizetti's *Lucrezia Borgia*, a part with which she was to be associated throughout her career. Based in London from 1858 onwards, Tietjens settled in Ivy Cottage, Grove End Road and starred in the first London performances of *The Sicilian Vespers, A Masked Ball, Faust, Medea, The Merry Wives of Windsor* and *The Force of Destiny*. In 1875 she was chosen to lay the foundation stone

112. *Thèrese Tietjens, soprano who lived in Grove End Road.*

of the never-to-be-built Grand National Opera House at the Embankment. She gave her last performance in 1877 – as Lucrezia Borgia – and fainted on stage immediately afterwards, from the terrible pain of the cancer that would eventually kill her. Notwithstanding her corpulent ungainliness, Tietjens proved to have a fine dramatic sense as well as a comprehensive repertoire. Despite her superstar status she was always willing to take minor parts in productions she approved and to play in commercially dubious works if she thought them of artistic merit.

Baritone **Sir Charles Santley** (1834-1922), the son of a music teacher, studied in Milan but resolutely refused advice to change his name to Santalini to advance his career. As a member of Mapleson's company he sang in the premiere of *The Flying Dutchman*, the first Wagner opera to be presented in London, and likewise starred in the first London performance of *Faust*. Santley also toured successfully in the USA, where he accepted an invitation to join the Carl Rosa Opera. Shaw, invariably waspish in his critical appraisals, acknowledged Santley's immense popularity, observing that he gave untutored audiences far better than most of them could recognise and, in a supremely well-turned simile, declared that Santley was to the concert platform what W.G. Grace was to the cricket-field. A devout Catholic, Santley was honoured by the Pope and also knighted in 1907. Santley lived at 4 Grove End Road.

The Irish singer **Allan James Foley** (1835-1899) had no reservations about promoting himself as Signor Foli. Originally a carpenter by trade, he trained in Italy and in 1865 was hired by Mapleson. He sang in London until 1887, presenting over sixty roles, and took part in numerous choral festivals in the provinces. Foley, listed as Giacomo Foli, is listed as resident at St Michael's Villa in Abbey Road, between Albert Terrace and Alexandra Road, 1868-73.

Zelia Trebelli (1838-1892) was another of Mapleson's proteges, singing alongside her friend and near neighbour Tietjens in the premiere performances of *Faust* and *The Force of Destiny*.

Born in Paris, she sang in Madrid and Berlin before making her London debut in 1862 in *Lucrezia Borgia*. Reviewing the London opera scene in 1877 George Bernard Shaw pronounced Trebelli to be "without a rival amongst contraltos or a superior amongst singers ... Mme. Trebelli alone combines the truest lyrical expression with a style and phrasing so perfect that the greatest virtuoso of the pianoforte or violin might profit by hearing her sing the works of Handel and Mozart". Not the least of his unalloyed praises was for this non-native speaker's complete mastery of English diction, a subject which became one of his lifelong obsessions. Having toured the United States with Mapleson in 1878, Trebelli returned to make her debut at the 'Met' in 1883, performing regularly there until her retirement in 1888. As capable an actress as Tietjens, she had an astonishing vocal range of two and a half octaves. She was married to the temperamental Italian tenor Alessandro Bettini, with whom she lived in Abbey Road.

Sophia Scalchi (1850-1922), a resident of Finchley Road, sang at Covent Garden from 1868 to 1890. After touring the United States with Mapleson in 1882, she returned the following year to sing at the opening performance of the New York Metropolitan Opera. This became her permanent operatic home from 1891 until her retirement in 1896. Shaw conceded that, as an actress, Scalchi possessed "a certain tragic grace" and as a singer was "generally efficient". Sometimes, however, her emotions got the better of her and on one occasion she was so paralysed with grief at the death of a favourite pet that she refused to take the stage.

The 'Yankee Diva' **Lillian Nordica** (1857-1914) was born in Maine and came to England at 21. She made her Italian debut in 1879, performed in Germany and Russia and then toured in her native America with Mapleson. Her Covent Garden debut did not come until 1887 but soon led to an engagement at Drury Lane for Augustus Harris and in 1894 to the part of Elsa in *Lohengrin* at Bayreuth. She lived at 27 Finchley Road.

FINDING A VOICE

Antoinette Sterling (1843-1904) perhaps deserved the style of 'Yankee Diva' even more than Nordica did. Born in New York State, she was brought up in a household so anti-British that, inspired by accounts of the Boston tea party, she swore she would never let tea pass her lips – and kept her word. Her prejudice did not, however, prevent her from settling in St John's Wood – she lived at 24 Marlborough Place – with her American singer husband. A forceful personality with strong views on many subjects, she initially rebelled against what she regarded as falling standards of public taste and insisted that she would only sing oratorios and German lieder. In 1877 she found the perfect vehicle for her talents in Sir Arthur Sullivan's *The Lost Chord* but thereafter became primarily associated with sentimental and moralising ballads. In matters of dress her personal convictions led her to refuse ever to wear low-cut dresses – or corsets. In her later years she became a fervent Christian Scientist.

Impresario **Carl Rosa** (1842-1889) was born in Hamburg and at twelve toured Europe as a violin prodigy. After studying in Leipzig and Paris, he toured in the United States, where he met and married the singer Euphrosyne Parepa and formed the Carl Rosa Opera Company. Following the early death of his wife in 1874, he opened his first London season in 1875, with *Figaro*, starring Santley. From 1883 he lived at 10 Warwick Crescent, Maida Hill.

Carl Rosa's principal tenor was another St John's Wood resident, **Joseph Maas** (1847-1886) who had begun his musical career as a boy chorister in Rochester Cathedral. Maas sang the name role in the first English performance of *Rienzi* and was much in demand to sing Handel at provincial festivals.

Composer **Mary Frances Allitsen** (1848-1912), commemorated in Allitsen Road (until 1938 Henry Street), was the daughter of bookseller John Bumpus. She lived at 20 Queen's Grove and adopted Allitsen as her pseudonym. Trained at the Guildhall School of Music, she made a late singing debut in 1882 and eventually became professor of singing at Blackheath Conservatoire but devoted her professional efforts mainly to composition. Her patriotic songs, vigorously interpreted by the singer Dame Clara Butt (who lived in nearby Elsworthy Road in Hampstead), enjoyed wide popularity. *There's a land* hit the right jingoistic note during the Boer War. But Allitsen also devised more subtle musical settings for poems by Tennyson and Heine and a series of four songs, based on Chinese verses, known as *A Lute of Jade* (1910). Her two-act opera, *Bindra the*

113. Allitsen Road before extensive demolition in 1949. It was named after the composer, Mary Allitsen. George Orwell taught Home Guard volunteers here at the drill hall, which has been converted into apartments.

Minstrel, was published in the year of her death but went unperformed. Her brothers John and Edward Bumpus became well-known distributors of sheet music and her sister Emma Allitsen was a proficient concert contralto.

VIOLIN VIRTUOSO

Joseph Joachim (1831-1907) was what one might call a periodic Londoner. A child prodigy who made his concert debut at eight, Joachim became a protégé of Mendelssohn and a friend of Brahms, whose music he introduced to the English public. From 1862 onwards he made annual visits to London and at some time lived in Grove End Road. Painted by Singer Sargent, feted by Alma-Tadema, Joachim received an honorary doctorate from Cambridge University in 1877 and he reciprocated by conducting the first English performance of Brahms's First Symphony.

LIGHTNING CONDUCTOR

No figure in the musical world better deserves the appellation 'larger than life' than the unsinkable **Sir Thomas Beecham** (1879-1961), a longtime resident of the Wood. As a young married man he lived in Upper Hamilton Terrace, moving with his

114. Sir Thomas Beecham.

115. Sir Thomas Beecham's house at 31 Grove End Road.

the following year he turned impresario and staged the first English performances of Strauss's *Der Rosenkavalier* and *Ariadne auf Naxos*. Knighted in 1914 at the early age of thirty-five, he succeeded to his father's baronetcy in 1916, the year in which he was appointed conductor to the Royal Philharmonic Society. By 1919, however, his personal and professional extravagances had driven him into bankruptcy. Undaunted, Beecham bounced back to conduct the New York Philharmonic in 1928, organise a London tribute to Delius in 1929 and in 1932 found the London Philharmonic. From 1941 to 1943 he was musical director of the Seattle Symphony Orchestra. In 1946 he returned to establish the Royal Philharmonic orchestra and in 1951 became principal conductor at Covent Garden.

second wife to Wellington Road, then living in Circus Road and finally settling at 31 Grove End Road. A child of privilege, thanks to a family fortune founded on pharmaceuticals, Beecham organised his first orchestra when he was just twenty, conducting Manchester's celebrated Hallé Orchestra soon afterwards. He made his conducting debut in the capital in 1905 and in 1909 established the Beecham Symphony Orchestra and

Beecham's bravura personal style was buttressed by a celebrated wit and a gift for brusque musical judgments. The harpsichord, Beecham opined, sounded "like two skeletons copulating on a tin roof"; he dismissed the third movement of Beethoven's Seventh Symphony as "like a lot of yaks jumping about" and summarised the performing arts of America as "a gigantic racket run by unscrupulous men for unhealthy women".

116. One of the lesser-known of St John's Wood's musical luminaries. Ernest Crampton of 10 Queen's Terrace, wrote songs for light entertainment.

PERMANENT ADDRESS

10, QUEEN'S TERRACE,
ST. JOHN'S WOOD, N.W.

ERNEST CRAMPTON'S

Original Songs sung by

"The Brownies" and "The Cigarettes"

. . . in their Entertainments . . .

Gavotte Song :— 'A HUNDRED YEARS AGO,'
Published by CARY & Co.,
Oxford Circus Avenue, London, W.

'MY CIGARETTE,'   'WILLIAM, JAMES and 'ENRY,'
'TERRORS TERRITORIAL,'
'WHEN YOU SAY GOOD-BYE.'   'IF EVERY ROSE,'
Published by ARCHERBERG HOPWOOD & CREW, Ltd.,
16, Mortimer Street, London, W.

'HEREAFTER'   'TWO SHORT SONGS,'
Published by LEONARD & Co., Oxford St., W.

'AT THE END OF THE WAY,'
Published by LUBLIN & Co., Mortimer Street, W.

'FICTION FOR THE FIRESIDE,'   *Words by Heslop.*
Published by REYNOLDS & Co., Berners Street, W.
Etc., Etc.

INSTRUMENTAL TO SUCCESS

Other musical luminaries who have lived in St John's Wood include **Dame Maggie Teyte** (1888-1976) who lived in a tiny modern house over a garage in Hamilton Terrace. She became one of the world's foremost interpreters of French song. Pianist **Dame Myra Hess** (1890-1965) was bombed out of her Carlton Hill home, and moved to Cavendish Close.

Maria Korchinska (1895-1979) managed, despite her aristocratic background, to escape retribution during the Bolshevik Revolution in her native Russia, and emigrated to London in 1926, where she settled into a strawberry pink cottage in Greville Road. Her many concert appearances included the first performance of Bax's *Fantasy Sonata* for viola and harp, which was dedicated to her.

THE WORLD'S MOST FAMOUS ZEBRA CROSSING

The house which formed the original core of the Abbey Road recording studios, originally no. 2 (promoted to no. 3 in 1872) was built in 1830 as a nine-bedroom mansion, complete with wine cellar, servants' quarters and a 250-foot garden. After the First World War it was converted into flats. Between 1929 and 1931 the building and adjoining properties were converted again by the newly-formed conglomerate Electrical and Musical Industries (EMI) to create the largest building then existing in the world to be devoted exclusively to sound recording. The first recording made at Abbey Road, on 12 November 1931, was Elgar's *Land of Hope and Glory*, with the London Symphony Orchestra conducted by the composer himself. This first Abbey Road session produced the first Abbey Road hit.

Abbey Road's unique place in the history of music recording has its own chroniclers and defies neat summary. Suffice to say that historic recordings made there range from Glenn Miller's *In the Mood* to Pink Floyd's *Dark Side of the Moon*, from Cliff Richard singing *Move It* to Cilla Black, personally conducted by composer Burt Bacharach, singing *Alfie*. There has also been a strong comedy connection. The 1960s satirical revue *Beyond the Fringe* was recorded at Abbey Road and so were humorous hit records by Rolf Harris, Charlie Drake and Peter Sellers and Sophia Loren. Film sound-

117. *The Abbey Road studios.*

tracks have long provided bread-and-butter work for London's army of talented session players. Recent Abbey Road examples have included *Raiders of the Lost Ark*, *Braveheart* and *Return of the Jedi*.

Most famously of all, Abbey Road is associated with the Beatles and their gifted mentor, the arranger (Sir) George Martin, who first came to the studios in 1950 as an oboist but was swiftly promoted to take charge of the Parlophone label. Between 1962 and 1970 the Beatles taped virtually all of their 200-plus recordings at Abbey Road, mainly in Studio 2. It was this association, and the 1969 album title, which changed the name of the building itself from the plain 'EMI Studios' to the 'Abbey Road Studios', a shrine of pilgrimage for Beatles fans world-wide. *That* photograph of the Fab Four traversing the zebra crossing outside was taken at 11.35 on Friday 8 August 1969 by freelance Iain Macmillan, balancing on a step-ladder, with a Hasselblad (using a 50mm wide-angle lens, aperture f22, at 1/500 sec.). Shot five, of six taken, was chosen, partly because it was the only one in which the Beatles were all in step and partly because it showed them walking *away* from the studios – hence sending a symbolic message about their professional relationship with the recording industry. This proved no empty gesture, *Abbey Road* being their last album.

Artists and Academicians

THE PIONEERS

The connection between the portraitist **George Romney** (1734-1802) and St John's Wood was, to be truthful, but brief and slight. In the last decade of his life Pine Apple Place on Maida Vale represented a rural retreat eagerly to be sought as a diversion from the pressures of life in fashionable Cavendish Square, where his sitters had famously included Emma, Lady Hamilton, the mistress of Lord Nelson. Romney's last years were clouded by bitterness at his failure to make a transition from portraiture to the newly fashionable and more grandiose field of 'History Painting' and he died insane.

The relationship of **John Sell Cotman** (1782-1842) with St John's Wood, by contrast, could not be more permanent, as his grave lies in the churchyard of what was, when he died, still St John's Wood Chapel. Cotman was the distinguished leader of the 'Norwich School' of watercolour painters. He came from Norwich to London at sixteen, returning to East Anglia in 1806. In 1833 he came back to London to teach drawing at newly-founded King's College; Dante Gabriel Rossetti was one of his pupils. In his last years Cotman developed an idiosyncratic technique of drawing in watercolour mixed with flour paste. The bleak severity of his later landscapes, however, brought little financial success.

In 1823 **John Jackson** RA (1778-1831) crowned a successful career of painting portraits of the aristocracy by moving into 16 (now 32) Grove End Road, where he died. Jackson's first effort had been to copy a portrait by Reynolds of the actor George Colman the Elder. A friend of Wilkie and Haydon, he also painted portraits of the actor Macready, the architect Sir John Soane and the sculptor John Flaxman. Despite his acknowledged competence and social connections Jackson never made more than £1,500 a year – which his contemporary Sir Thomas Lawrence once charged for a single picture. In later years Jackson's consistent generosity to Wesleyan causes considerably impoverished him. It is perhaps then ironic that he was buried in the Anglican churchyard of St John's Wood Chapel.

The attachment of **Benjamin Robert Haydon** (1786-1846) to St John's Wood and its neighbourhood was more enduring than Romney's but his ending was, if anything, even more tragic. Art

118. *The memorial to John Sell Cotman in the burial ground of St John's Wood Church.*

119. *Benjamin Haydon; pencil and chalk drawing by G.H. Harlow, 1816.*

historian Jeremy Maas has summarised Haydon's career in the single word 'ludicrous', noting that "on the rare occasions when fortune smiled on him, his headstrong intransigence rejected its benefits". William Hazlitt observed of Haydon's *Judgment of Solomon* "Why did you paint it so large? A small canvas might have concealed your faults." But Haydon was determined to paint 'Great works and great works only' – in the most literal sense; his *Raising of Lazarus* measured fourteen feet by twenty-one feet. In 1820 he exhibited an enormous canvas of *Christ's Entry into Jerusalem* at the Egyptian Hall in Piccadilly. Admissions at a shilling a time, plus sales of catalogues, brought in the not ungratifying sum of £1,760 – which proved not nearly enough to offset the debts incurred during the six years it had taken him to complete it. Haydon's hubris was compounded by a bad temper, bad money management and bad luck. He consistently antagonised patrons, was imprisoned three times for debt and endured the death of five of his children. He finally cut his throat – *and* shot himself in the head – at a house in Lisson Grove, leaving behind yet more debts, a wife and six more children. Seven years later his diaries were published – 27 volumes of marvellously observed gossip and anecdote, recorded in a sparkling prose, iridescent with delicate barbs – a revelation of his life's missing masterpiece.

Charles Robert Leslie (1794-1859) was born in London of American parents who returned to Philadelphia, where he was brought up, but he eventually settled at 12 Pine Apple Place (subsequently 54 Maida Vale). He enjoyed much success in painting humorous and anecdotal scenes. These were chiefly drawn from literary sources which not only included the usual British authors but also Cervantes and Molière. He was, therefore, one of that influential group of early Victorian painters who taught the British public to search out the detail in a composition and treat a painting as though it were a two-dimensional novel in a rectangle. In 1838 he enjoyed an unexpected success with his painting of the coronation of Queen Victoria. It had not been commissioned by the new monarch but she bought it anyway, for 600 guineas. Leslie, who moved to 2 Abercorn Place in 1847, became a Professor at the Royal Academy Schools in that year. His son G.D. Leslie was a member of the St John's Wood Clique and also acted as a painting assistant to Landseer.

Thomas Shotter Boys (1803-1874) was a watercolourist who produced many views of the cities of northern France and Belgium, which reached a wider market in the 1830s via the new printing process of chromolithography. Returning to London in 1837, he produced a series of tinted lithographs of the capital in 1841. Aesthetically speaking the rest of his working life is reckoned to represent an extended anti-climax, partly because he was plagued by ill health. Boys lived in Acacia Road.

LANDSEER

Sir Edwin Landseer (1803-1873) no longer enjoys the esteem which was *almost* universal during his lifetime (Constable thought his work was ridiculous). The *Stag at Bay* and *The Monarch of the Glen* have become visual cliches of mid-Victorian bourgeois taste. John Steegman in his *Victorian Taste* noted witheringly that he "could be a surprisingly good painter, though he seldom revealed the fact".

Landseer lived at 1 St John's Wood Road from 1828 until his death in 1873. His first home was a rustic cottage by Punker's Barn, later demolished to make way for a house which was also "small but rather aristocratic and dignified in aspect." The dining-room was tiny but there was a billiard room and two more very large rooms, one used as a studio, the other to store painterly props. The spacious garden and stables were also occasionally used to accommodate animals, both alive and dead, which the artist needed as models. (One of his most celebrated commissions was to design the lions which adorn the base of Nelson's Column – for which he used as a model a real, dead lion, delivered from Regent's Park Zoo by cab.) The

120. Sir Edwin Landseer.

The House
Front elevation

The Studio.

Room in which
Sir Edwin
died.

Sir
Edwins
favourite
Seat

The Garden front.

Holland Tringham

121. *Landseer's house in St John's Wood Road, built by Thomas Cubitt, who also built Osborne House
on the Isle of Wight for Queen Victoria.*

122. *Landseer painting his famous picture, 'Monarch of the Glen.'*

household was run by Landseer's sister, Jessie, herself a talented miniaturist and etcher, "a meek, amiable little body who looked after her brother's house in a very quiet and unostentatious way". She was assisted by an eccentric butler, Bishop, who routinely informed all callers – including, on one occasion, the Prince Consort – that 'Sir Hedwin' was not at home.

Landseer's brother, Thomas, an eminent engraver, lived nearby, at 10a Cunningham Place, from 1841 to 1876 and at 11 Grove End Road from 1876 to 1880. Thomas's son, George (1834-76) produced watercolours of India.

Landseer's professional admirers included his French contemporaries Gericault and Delacroix. *The Old Shepherd's Chief Mourner*, exhibited at the Royal Academy in 1837, which depicts a faithful dog leaning against his master's coffin in a bare peasant hut, was extravagantly praised by the youthful aesthete John Ruskin in his *Modern Painters. Blackwood's Magazine* declared of Landseer in 1840 "His are not mere animals; they tell a story. You see them not only alive, but you see their biography, and know what they do, and if the

expression be allowed, what they think."

In later years Landseer's work reflected the increasing morbidity of his mood, depicting nature as savage rather than sublime. *Man Proposes, God Disposes,* painted in 1864, illustrates this tendency well – two polar bears in an Arctic wasteland savage the wreckage of Sir John Franklin's disastrous 1845 expedition to find the North-West Passage. In 1865 Landseer refused election as President of the Royal Academy. Chronic alcoholism and a traumatic railway accident sadly hastened the death of a man renowned in his prime for his kindness, hospitality, and polished manners. "The most popular painter England ever had" was honoured with burial beside Reynolds and Turner in St Paul's.

FRITH

The crowded canvases of **William Powell Frith** (1819-1909) were sneeringly dismissed in a sentence by Oscar Wilde – "he has elevated art to the level of photography". Frith, who rather raucously professed a total indifference to the opinions of professional critics, felt that particular gibe keenly enough to mock Wilde and his 'aesthetic' hangers-on in a painting of *The Private View at the Royal Academy* (1881). Wilde's barb was, however, closer to the mark than even he may have expected for, in painstakingly assembling his 1858 master-piece, *Derby Day*, Frith made extensive use of specially commissioned photographs of the fa-mous Epsom grandstand and the milling crowds in front of it.

Frith trained at the well-known drawing-school run by Henry Sass in Charlotte Street, just off Tottenham Court Road. His classmates included Millais, future President of the Royal Academy, and Edward Lear, who was to prove a poet of sublime nonsense rhymes and an accomplished watercolourist of Middle Eastern scenes. Having painted portraits of Lincolnshire gentry, and vainly sought inspiration in the works of Goldsmith and Scott, Frith found his professional salvation when he set himself to produce elaborately detailed, large scale compositions which reproduced a 'slice of life'. Elected RA in 1853, Frith enjoyed his first public triumph the following year with *Ramsgate Sands*, which was complimented by Queen Victo-ria herself. *Derby Day* not only gained the ap-proval of the more discerning eye of Prince Albert but also achieved the singular distinction of being railed off to protect it from an admiring public, the first time this had happened at a Summer Exhibition since 1822. This *coup de théâtre* was, in fact, a piece of shrewd public relations, skillfully engineered by the art dealer Gambart, who cashed in handsomely on the painting by buying the reproduction copyright for £1,500 and having it mass-produced as an engraving.

The Railway Station (1862), modelled on Pad-dington and featuring both a dramatic arrest and the artist himself, sold for the fabulous sum of £4,500. The following year Frith was honoured by a royal commission to paint an official record of the marriage of the Prince of Wales to Princess Alexandra of Denmark. Prostrate with grief for her beloved Albert, parsimonious Queen Victoria remained an exacting patron, at least in regard to the financial aspect of the relationship. The fee was to be a handsome £3,000 but, having seen Frith's previous work, the sovereign was confi-dent that this would guarantee her the largest number of recognisable individual portraits for the least feasible expenditure.

What one critic characterised as Frith's "ill-advised attempts to rival Hogarth" enabled him to live well, keeping a studio at 10 Pembridge Villas, Bayswater, and a separate house at no. 16. He once boasted that "my work has never been interrupted, I am thankful to say, by illness, and I never allowed it to be interrupted by anything else" - which was not entirely true, as he also found time to procreate nineteen children.

In 1896 Frith moved into a modest cul-de-sac semi-detached villa at 114 Clifton Hill, where he passed the last decade of his life, a genial, white-haired old gentleman, still painting – but strictly for his own satisfaction. Frith's compositions, although hugely popular with the general public, had never won the approbation of the cognoscenti and, unlike Alma-Tadema, the artist also lived long enough to see their selling price crash as well.

TWILIGHT OF A PRE-RAPHAELITE

By the time **Ford Madox Brown** (1821-1893) had moved into 1 St Edmund's Terrace he had already attained the status of a Grand Old Man of British art. His best known works, *The Last of England* and *Work*, are justly honoured as masterpieces of Victorian genre. The former is a bitter comment on emigration, the latter an allegorical celebration of labour in which 'brain workers' Thomas Carlyle and F.D. Maurice, founder of the Working Men's College, contemplate hefty navvies digging up the road at Hampstead. Both paintings were begun in 1852, the former being completed in 1856, the latter not until 1865.

Stricken with gout and the after-effects of a stroke, Brown, ever a prickly character, was lat-terly reduced to pondering the purposes of art rather than pursuing it with his former vigour. In ordering the decor of the house he was assisted by the Scottish architect Arthur Mackmurdo (1851-1942), a disciple of William Morris. The drawing-room featured Japanese gold-embossed paper wall-coverings. The first floor studio was embellished with gilded leather and dark green paintwork and boasted an armchair which had once belonged to Dante Rossetti. In July 1888, by way of a house-warming, Brown invited over two hundred guests to a Sunday afternoon entertainment. Thirty actually turned up, but what the guest-list lacked in quantity it made up for in eminence. Alma-Tadema came. So did Holman Hunt. William Morris, typically, was the first to arrive and the last to go. That same year Brown was still strong enough to take part in the first showing of the Arts and Crafts Exhibition Society, which was dedi-cated to Morris's ethic of art-before-profit.

After Brown's wife died in 1890 he was reduced to a half-life, sitting in his studio for hours at a time, alone and motionless, at other times wan-dering the house, vainly looking for her. Occa-sionally he would rouse himself to continue work on a series of historical murals, commissioned for Manchester's new Town Hall, which had occu-

123. *Ford Madox Brown's painting 'Work'. It depicts Thomas Carlyle and F.D. Maurice watching workmen digging up the road near Heath Street, Hampstead.*

pied him for twenty years. In 1892 he managed to attend a Lord Mayor's Mansion House banquet to honour 'Art and Literature' and also received his final artistic commission. Ironically, in view of his age and half-demented state, it was to design the set and costumes for a production by Sir Henry Irving of *King Lear*. In 1896 a biography of Ford Madox Brown was published by his grandson Ford Herman Hueffer (1873-1939), who had shared his grandfather's house in St. Edmund's Terrace. Better known as Ford Madox Ford, he was to become a prolific author and influential promoter of new writers.

VARIOUS VICTORIANS

St John's Wood was home to so many Victorian painters that many must be mentioned but briefly, and even more omitted altogether. In his evidence to the Parliamentary Select Committee on Arts and Manufactures in 1836 Benjamin Haydon reckoned that there were over two thousand professional artists in London. As only forty could achieve the

eminence of becoming a Royal Academician at any one time the fact that so many St John's Wood residents achieved this status represents an emphatic endorsement of their standing in the eyes of contemporaries.

In 1840 **John Rogers Herbert** (1810-1890) followed the architect A.W.N. Pugin into Catholicism, abandoning genre paintings for painstaking depictions of Biblical scenes. Herbert lived opposite Landseer, with whom he used to play billiards. A native of Maldon, Essex he consistently affected a French accent, which, when abruptly dropped in moments of surprise or anger, caused much hilarity among his younger contemporaries. All Herbert's three sons, Arthur, Cyril and Wilfred, grew up to become painters.

When Herbert moved to Kilburn in 1869 his house in St John's Wood Road was taken by the Scottish artist **John Pettie** (1839-1893), an honorary member of the St John's Wood Clique, whose dashing historical compositions made him 'the painterly equivalent of Dumas'. Pettie had come to London "with some idea of avenging Flodden, but I soon found everybody so kind, so hearty and so hospitable, that the idea grew fainter and fainter every day and after a while it disappeared ..." It was on the doorstep of this house that, when they learned of Pettie's election as ARA, the Cliquists hastily assembled to welcome his return by crowning him with a wreath of laurels snatched from the garden, to the accompaniment of *See, the Conquering Hero Comes* played on a comb and paper.

Artists often spent years experimenting with different subjects until they finally defined their own market niche, which they then mined assiduously. **Frederick Goodall** (1822-1904), an occupant of 62 Avenue Road, concentrated on Middle Eastern scenes, then switched to fairies. **Thomas Sidney Cooper** (1803-1902), who lived at Portland Terrace, Wellington Road and then at 16 Wellington Road, remained a formula artist until his death at ninety-nine, having established an all-time record for continuous exhibiting at the RA – 266 pictures, all animals. Contented cattle were his favourite subject but on one occasion he decided to branch out by attempting to depict a cavalry charge at the battle of Waterloo. Cooper's research for this project included hiring "a strong cab-horse to be galloped up and down in front of my house in Wellington Road", while the artist sat on his garden wall trying to capture its motion with pencil and pad. Afterwards he took the exhausted nag into his garden to sketch "veins and muscles ... fully developed from his exertions". These proceedings occasioned much hilarity among the neighbourhood's other cabmen but did the horse no good at all. Cooper refused to buy the exhausted nag but did agree to give its disgruntled owner his exclusive custom thereafter.

Sir John Tenniel (1820-1914) is best remembered for his immortal illustrations to the first published editions of *Alice in Wonderland* (1866) and *Alice Through the Looking Glass* (1870) but in the 1850s, when he was living in Portsdown Road, Maida Vale, he was contributing political cartoons to *Punch*, an association which continued until 1901.

Edwin Long RA (1829-1891), of Marlborough Hill, specialised in depicting scenes from ancient Egypt or showing early Christian martyrdoms. In 1875 his *Babylonian Marriage Market* went for seven thousand guineas, setting a contemporary record for the work of a living artist. **John Swan** (1847-1910) excelled in representing the big cats of the conveniently adjacent Regent's Park Zoo – suitably transplanted to jungle backgrounds - and had the knack of investing them with a genuinely predatory air of menace. He lived at 3 Acacia Road, 1889-1904.

John MacWhirter (1839-1911) excelled in Scottish and Alpine landscapes. After travelling extensively, from Norway to Sicily and from Turkey to the USA, MacWhirter finally settled in London in 1869, living first at 1 Titchfield Villas. Success enabled him to build an imposing mansion and studio at 1 Abbey Road, opposite the house of Alma-Tadema, where he lived from 1888 until his death. Portraits of MacWhirter were painted by both his friend and fellow Scot Pettie and by the sculptor Onslow Ford.

ALMA-TADEMA

Art historian Mario Amaya has epitomised Sir **Lawrence Alma-Tadema** (1836-1912) as "the most ridiculed painter of the nineteenth century, as well as the least written about." *The Oxford Companion to Art* notes sniffily " His remarkable social and financial success has yet to be endorsed by posterity as an artistic one." Perhaps – but posterity still provides a steady market for Alma-Tadema's elaborate compositions, though nowadays they are invariably and prolifically reproduced in the form of posters, postcards and calendars.

Dutch by birth but trained in Belgium, both as an artist and an archaeologist, Alma-Tadema exhibited his first canvas at the age of fifteen. On honeymoon in Italy in 1863 he devoted days to sketching the ruins of Pompeii. Shortly afterwards in Paris he met the influential art-dealer

124. Lawrence Alma-Tadema.

125.   Alma-Tadema's house in Grove End Road today.

126.   The panelled hallway of Alma-Tadema's house in Grove End Road.   Between 1885 and 1895 Alma-Tadema spent £70,000 on beautifying his house.   His architect, Philip Calderon's son Alfred, demolished 80% of Tissot's former residence in the course of this refurbishment.

127.   Three panels in Alma-Tadema's Townshend House.

128.   The entrance to Alma-Tadema's house in Grove End Road.

129. Alma-Tadema's studio in Grove End Road.

130. A recent photograph of Alma-Tadema's house in Grove End Road.

Gambart, who launched his work in England, where it found a ready market. In 1870, after the death of his first wife, Alma-Tadema settled in London, married an Englishwoman, Miss Epps, and became a British citizen in 1873. What more natural than that he should gravitate to St John's Wood, not only renowned as a colony of artists, but also the place where Gambart lived in style, not to say splendour, at 62 Avenue Road. Initially Alma-Tadema lived at 17 Titchfield Terrace, then at Townshend House and finally at 44 (in his day 17) Grove End Road, where he annexed Tissot's former residence to his own.

By his exquisite rendering of gold, jewels, silks, furs, marble and human flesh, Alma-Tadema precisely satisfied Victorian bourgeois taste for material richness. Brilliantly painted light-reflecting surfaces and meticulously researched architectural detail were to become characteristic hallmarks of the world of classical antiquity which he depicted with both flair and exactitude. His collection of photographs of Roman and Greek statues, buildings and artefacts, now deposited with the University of Birmingham, ran to 168 volumes. When Irving commissioned him to design the scenery for his 1880 production of *Coriolanus*, Alma-Tadema stunned the critics by correctly reproducing *Etruscan* settings and surpassed even this with his brilliant pioneering use of electric lighting to achieve the effects of dawn and moonlight.

A sociable man, who liked sport, dancing and music, Alma-Tadema could well afford to host celebrated Monday 'At Homes', where the imposing entrance to his house, incorporating a bronze surround cast from the doorway of the house of Eumachia in Pompeii, accurately foreshadowed the sumptuousness that lay within – Persian tiles, stained glass, a brass staircase and panels painted by such contemporaries of the artist as Lord Leighton, Sir Edward Poynter and John Singer Sargent. An 'autograph piano', inlaid with ivory and mother-of-pearl, featured parchment panels bearing the signatures of artists who had performed for the entertainment of the artist's guests – the pianist Paderewski, the violin maestro Joachim and the singer Sir Charles Santley.

Writing in the year of the artist's death A.M. Eyre wonderingly described Alma-Tadema's house at its apogee and on the eve of the dispersal of its wonders:-

> "The studio is of unusually large proportions, with a domed ceiling filled with amber glass. The walls are panelled with grey-green Siena marble; the apse and dome are covered with aluminium leaf; the tapestries and upholsteries produce a quiet grey tone ... In the atrium leading from the studio the ceiling is a copy from one in Pompeii, and the window represents a sun of onyx. In one room are choice treasures from China and Japan, in another are cabinets and brasses of fine Netherlands workmanship. From a balcony on a landing one overlooks a Roman scene, with its marble basin and playing fountain ... The whole bears testimony to the mind and temperament of no ordinary man."

In retrospect it is clear that Alma-Tadema had a uniquely *explosive* relationship with St John's Wood. His first foray, to Gambart's fancy-dress ball in 1866, ended dramatically when an unsuspected build-up of gas led to an explosion which killed a maid-servant and left the first Mrs. Alma-Tadema in a state of severe shock. Townshend House, the artist's first home in the Wood, had to be virtually rebuilt following the damage inflicted by the Regent's Canal explosion of 1874. On that occasion Alma-Tadema himself was not in residence, although his two children were and had to be hurried across the park to take refuge in the house of his relative, Dr Epps. The Grove End Road mansion was therefore embellished with many fittings brought over bodily from the ruins of Townshend House. Once hailed as "the most beautiful house in London", it is now in even sorrier condition than its former owner's artistic reputation.

THE NEXT GENERATION

J. William Waterhouse (1849-1917), who lived at 10 Hall Road, 1901-07, was a disciple of Alma-Tadema and almost as successful, at least in terms of popular appeal. The painter Charles Hemming goes further – "it would be unjust to devalue his pictures by equation with Alma-Tadema's. Waterhouse's paintings are more earthly ... not Greek ideals but delicate portraits of the Surrey landscape. Landscape painting could go no further in the poetic adoration of the earth." Waterhouse's painting of *The Lady of Shallot* was the Tate Gallery's top-selling postcard in the mid-1990s.

E. J. Gregory (1850-1909) was one of those artists who worked half a lifetime to become an overnight success. His 1898 painting *Boulter's Lock - Sunday Afternoon*, an immensely detailed, crowded but harmonious evocation of river recreation, represented the fruit of years of painstaking labour. Hailed by the *Art Journal* as "a picture for which his public have long been waiting", it was admired by Sargent and guaranteed the artist's election as RA. Gregory lived at 6 Abercorn Place from 1879-88, and at 8 Greville Place 1897-1903.

Sir George Clausen (1852-1944), a pupil of Edwin Long, moved to St John's Wood in the 1880s and was at 61 Carlton Hill 1906-12. He managed to straddle the widening divide between the Royal Academy, where he became Professor of Painting in 1908, and such emerging 'progressive' movements as the New English Art Club of 1886, of which he was a founder member. He painted many rural scenes in Essex but also designed posters for the London, Midland and Scottish Railway.

Frank Dicksee (1853-1928) specialised in pictures of chivalry and romance, such as King Arthur, Romeo and Juliet or Tannhauser. He lived in Greville House, Greville Place.

Walter Dendy Sadler (1854-1923) lived successively at 34, 28 and 44 Finchley Road. He was a co-founder of the St John's Wood Art Club, specialising in humorous and sentimental scenes, usually set in the Regency period, which reached a wide public through cheap engravings.

William Strang (1859-1921), who lived at 20 Hamilton Terrace, was another Scot by birth and a star pupil of Legros at the Slade School of Art. A master of the woodcut and an accomplished producer of portrait drawings, he is chiefly known for his 747 etchings, most made as illustrations for literary classics such as *Don Quixote*, *The Rime of the Ancient Mariner* or the *Short Stories* of Rudyard Kipling.

Of Danish descent, **Maurice William Greiffenhagen** (1862-1931) – 'Griffin' to his intimates – regularly illustrated the adventure stories of H. Rider Haggard. Although he lived at 12 Loudoun Road, Greiffenhagen also managed to hold down the post of head of the life department at the Glasgow School of Art from 1906 to 1929. Apart from portraits, he also specialised in large-scale decoration, being responsible for pavilions at the celebrated Paris Expo of 1925.

Cartoonist **Phil May** (1864-1903) began his career at the age of twelve painting scenery at Leeds theatre and tried acting – he played the cat in *Dick Whittington* – before, like his semi-fictional mentor, trying his fortune in London. It was a caricature of the actors Irving, Bancroft and Toole which first brought May to public attention. Bancroft was so impressed he bought the original and Pinero and the Prince of Wales bought copies. May then emigrated to Australia for health reasons and from 1885 to 1888 contributed some 900 drawings to the *Sydney Bulletin*. After studying art in Paris on his way back to England, May settled in St John's Wood. Sociable and generous to a fault, he became a regular habitué of the Eyre Arms Tavern. Apart from contributing caricatures and humorous scenes of Cockney life to illustrated magazines such as *Punch*, May also published annual and occasional albums such as *Phil May's Gutter-snipes* (1896). His cartooning achieved a striking simplicity of line, much admired by the ultra-critical Whistler. May died at 5 Melina Place, not yet forty.

Phil May's all-too-brief career at *Punch*, overlapped with that of **(Sir) Bernard Partridge** (1861-1945) who joined the magazine in 1891, having been an actor with Irving. Talented enough as a 'straight' artist to design stained glass and to exhibit

Phil May in his studio   C. J. Taylor 1898

131. *Phil May at work in his studio.*

132. Maurice Greiffenhagen, painted by A.D. McCormick.

at the Royal Academy, Partridge remained senior cartoonist at *Punch* for the best part of half a century. He lived at 11 Marlborough Road.

THE TWENTIETH CENTURY

The first women to be made members of the Royal Academy, Angelica Kauffmann and Mary Moser, were among its founders in 1768. The next to be so honoured, over a century and a half later, was **Dame Laura Knight** (1877-1970). Born Laura Johnson in Long Eaton, Derbyshire and trained in Nottingham, she met her husband, painter Harold Knight (1874-1961), when they were both students. After a brief spell at 1 and 2 Queen's Road, her base was to be at 16 Langford Place. When working in oils Laura Knight's favourite subjects included gypsies, the ballet and the circus but she also painted notable watercolour landscapes. She was created Dame in 1929 and RA in 1936. Harold, a conservative portraitist, was elected RA in 1937. In 1965 Dame Laura became the first woman to be honoured by the Royal Academy with a retrospective exhibition of her life's work. Notwithstanding this unprecedented compliment *The Oxford Companion to Art* is severe in its judgment – "Her work was extremely competent by academic standards of technique but was judged to be lacking in aesthetic taste and sensibility."

Cosmopolitan, half-Austrian, half-Czech **Oskar Kokoschka** (1886-1980) trained in Vienna and worked as an illustrator of avant-garde magazines in Berlin, where he established a reputation as a portraitist of compelling psychological insight. Seriously injured in the war in 1915, he taught at Dresden Academy from 1919 to 1924, then travelled widely before settling in Eyre Court, Wellington Road in 1938 and turning to landscapes and allegorical compositions inspired by classical themes. Kokoschka also painted many pictures of his adopted city, and especially of the Thames, the earliest, a series of eleven, dating from 1925-6, the last from 1970. In 1967 he recorded his repeated efforts "to capture the Thames ... the artery of life flowing from century to century...". Though honoured by the Arts Council in 1962 with a retrospective of his work, the British remained reluctant to buy his paintings.

Ivon Hitchens (1893-1979) studied at the St John's Wood School of Art while living at home with his parents in 1911 and then at the Royal Academy under Sir William Orpen. From 1919 until he was bombed out in 1940 he kept a studio at 169 Adelaide Road, Hampstead. Migrating to live near Petworth, Sussex, in a caravan embedded in a positive jungle of a garden, Hitchens came to concentrate on distinctive 'abstract landscapes' of the surrounding countryside, although he was equally adept at painting nudes or murals.

Meredith Frampton (1894-1984), the son of sculptor Sir George Frampton, grew up in St John's Wood and after Westminster School also attended the St John's Wood School of Art before proceeding to the Royal Academy School, where his medal-winning career was interrupted by military service in the Great War. From 1915 to 1918 Frampton was involved in the visually exacting task of cartographic interpretation from aerial reconnaissance photographs. It was an experience which was to influence his artistic career decisively, imbuing his portraits with an extreme precision and an almost palpable stillness. His best-known portrait was of George VI when still Duke of York; the sitter came to Frampton's St John's Wood studio in a taxi in the full glory of the uniform of an Admiral of the Fleet. Commissioned by Barnardo's orphanage, of which the future king was patron, the painting was acquired by the National Portrait Gallery in 1998.

Elected RA in 1942, Frampton was bombed out of his studio in the course of the war. His career was abruptly terminated in 1945 by a deterioration in his eyesight which made it impossible for him to achieve the fineness of finish which had become his trademark. Decamping to Wiltshire, where he threw himself into decorating a house he had built in the style of a seventeenth-century chateau, Frampton had the belated consolation of being rediscovered in the decade before his death by the critical avant-garde of Paris and hailed as "an unjustly overlooked master".

The Gridirons

*" The St John's Wood Clique - what memories
the name awakens! What sterling good fellows.
What high hopes! What camaraderie! Shall we
ever look upon the like of that artistic Brotherhood again? "*
Alan Montgomery Eyre: *Saint John's Wood*
(1913)

Eyre's enthusiastic invocation of a 'Brotherhood'
is apposite. The seven founder members of the
St John's Wood Clique (the SJWC) may well, when
they came together in 1862, have seen themselves
as both imitators and satirists of the celebrated
Pre-Raphaelite Brotherhood, which was founded
in 1848, when they all would have been children.
There are, indeed, many similarities between the
two groupings. Both consisted of young artists,
born within a few years of each other, who pledged
to collaborate in the interests of aesthetic excellence. The SJWC were led by Philip Hermogenes
Calderon (1833-98), son of a Spanish Catholic priest
who had turned Protestant and became Professor
of Spanish at King's College, London. Both groups
regarded themselves, and were regarded by avant-
garde critical opinion, as 'coming men'. There
remains, however, one critical distinction. The
Pre-Raphaelite Brotherhood numbered among its
ranks names which are honoured to this day for
their artistic achievements but the most enduring
legacy of the SJWC is a painting of a fictional
incident from the English Civil Wars entitled *"And
When Did You last See Your Father?"* – which came
to be derided as a classic example of the sentimental crassness of so much Victorian genre painting.
The fate of the SJWC was to be the reverse of their
French contemporaries, the early Impressionists
– revered in their lifetimes only to be reviled
within a generation.

Five of the seven founders of the Clique had
studied at Leigh's Academy of Drawing in
Newman Street, a turning off the north side of
Oxford Street. Calderon and Henry Stacy Marks
(1829-98) had also studied together under Picot in
Paris in 1851-53. When the group was established
in 1862 Calderon, Stacy Marks, John Evan
Hodgson (1831-95), George A. Storey (1834-1919)
and George D. Leslie (1835-1921were already living in St John's Wood. David Wilkie Wynfield
(1837-87) – named for his great uncle, the eminent
Academician Sir David Wilkie – and W. F. Yeames
(1835-1918) were living nearby in Paddington.
Yeames, after marrying Anne Wynfield, grand-
niece of Sir David Wilkie, in 1865, moved to the

133. Philip Hermogenes Calderon.

house at 4 Grove End Road previously occupied
by the singer George Santley and renamed it Acomb
Lodge. George Leslie lived only four doors away
and Calderon next door but one to him at Iveston
Lodge. Storey lived in Marlborough Place.

The members of the Clique pledged themselves
to a regime of rigorous mutual criticism. As
Calderon put it himself idealistically – "We have
all of us now to work together, and do our very
best, not caring who is first or last, but helping
each other so that all may come out strong. The
better each man's picture the better for all." To
symbolize the iron integrity of their joint purpose
the Clique adopted as their badge an icon – the
gridiron – and a motto 'Ever on Thee'. A.M. Eyre
interpreted the adoption of this symbol as "de-
scriptive of their object, which was, while continuing to be the best of friends, to criticise each other's
works in the frankest and most unsparing manner". Being ' Ever on Thee ' presumably implied
a willingness to be challenged perpetually. Both
icon and motto admit of a further layer of symbolic
reference, relating to Calderon's cultural and family
origins, the gridiron being the badge of St Lawrence, patron saint of Spain, who was martyred
by grilling – a method of torture also used by the

134. George Storey and sitter in his studio at 19 St John's Wood Road. Notice the fashionable oriental screen.

135. The St John's Wood Clique symbol and motto: 'Ever on Thee'.

Spanish Inquisition, and hence also an indirect reference to the religious tradition from which Calderon's father had detached himself by apostasy and emigration.

Apart from their solemn commitment to the high purposes of 'ART', the members of the Clique were notably distinguished for their addiction to practical jokes, silly songs, spoof sermons, cartoons, croquet and dressing up in historical costumes. Much time, effort and expense was invested in country excursions – to eat chops and sausages and play bowls at The Spotted Dog in Neasden, to take the train to St Albans and dine at the Peahen, to swim at Cassiobury Park, to travel in a hired omnibus to Richmond and there to consume sherry and bitters, tea, oysters and sauterne, champagne and coffee, finishing with 'swizzle', a heated concoction based on brandy and demerara sugar. Members of the group sometimes also took country holidays together, at Swanage, at Hambleden, at Wargrave and at Hever Castle – the last of which they nearly burned down after inadvertently setting light to a chimney in which an unsuspected jackdaw's nest was lodged.

136. A depiction of the St John's Wood Clique by Frederick Walker, RA.

The Sunday mornings of one winter were passed in decorating the walls of Hodgson's painting-room at 5 (now 10) Hill Road with near life-size Shakespearean subjects and scenes and portraits of the Hodgsons in Elizabethan rig-out.

Another common bond was the association of the Clique with the Dudley Gallery from 1864 to 1882. Five of the Clique were involved in selecting works for exhibition there. Their most talented discovery was Elizabeth Thompson, Lady Butler (1846-1933), who specialized in military scenes from the Crimean and Napoleonic wars which were both meticulous in detail and bravura in composition. Queen Victoria insisted on buying her picture of *The Roll Call* (1874) from its original purchaser, a Manchester manufacturer; but the Royal Academy still denied her even the status of ARA.

All seven members of the St John's Wood Clique eventually became Associate or full Members of the Royal Academy. They also made lots of money. In 1877 Yeames's *Amy Robsart* went for £1,000 – enough to have bought two dozen Gainsboroughs at the then going rate. The same artist's *And When Did You Last See Your Father?*, evidently evaluated as a contemporary masterpiece, was purchased for Liverpool's Walker Art Gallery only a year

after it opened. Sharing a common interest in genre and historical subjects, each of the Cliquists came to develop his own special interests, the common thread of which was escapism into a prettified past. The Cliquists were obsessed with literal verisimilitude and, in terms of lasting reputation, what they would have considered an essential proof of their professionalism in fact proved their undoing. As Bevis Hillier put it,

> "Like historical novelists, they tended to sabotage the illusion they were trying to create by overdoing the trimmings – the oriels, lattices, drawbridges, portcullises and gingerbread booths."

Stacy Marks, a confirmed practical joker, often gave a humorous slant to his canvases, enjoying early success with a work on the theme of 'Toothache in the Middle Ages'; he also became an accomplished painter of animals, as well as keeping a personal entourage of parakeets and mynah birds which also figured in his compositions. Hodgson's career took a decisive turn following a visit to North Africa in 1868, after which he focused heavily on 'Oriental' subjects, eventually becoming Professor of Painting at the Royal Academy (1882-95). Leslie's passion was for the

137. Mr and Mrs Hodgson, as depicted by Philip Calderon on a fresco.

landscape of the Thames valley. Storey turned to portraiture. Calderon's picture '*Broken Vows*' (1857) brought him an early reputation and, from its widespread reproduction as a cheap engraving, a useful windfall. In 1867 he was the only English artist to be awarded a gold medal at the Paris International Exhibition; although the fact that he had been born at Poitiers might have had some slight bearing on the French judges' interest in his work. In the 1870s he, too, turned to the safe and remunerative field of portraiture and from 1887 as Keeper of the Royal Academy, managed the RA Schools. Yeames, who had studied under the London-based German watercolourist George Scharf, specialised in historical scenes set in the sixteenth and seventeenth centuries, as did Wynfield, who inadvertently achieved a further, if indirect, distinction, as the man who introduced the middle-aged Julia Margaret Cameron (1815-79) to the art of photography. Cameron took from Wynfield the initially controversial notion that pictures taken deliberately 'out of focus' could gain aesthetic strength and went on to make impressionistic portraits of Victorian luminaries such as Carlyle, Tennyson, Browning, Darwin, which are now revered as being of epochal significance in the development of photography as an art.

The seven founder members of the Clique were later joined by a loose penumbra of associates, a number of whom enjoyed greater success than they ever did. Gifted, versatile Val Prinsep (1834-1904), became seriously rich through an advantageous marriage and ended his career as Professor of Painting at the Royal Academy. Once a fellow-student of George du Maurier in Paris, Prinsep was the model for the character of Taffy in the cult play that made du Maurier's fortune all too late – *Trilby*. Another fringe member of the Clique, Fred Walker (1840-75) was the model for Little Billee in the same play. Walker, another graduate of Leigh's Academy and the RA Schools, became one of the foremost magazine illustrators of the 1860s, before switching to watercolours and oils. His early death, from TB, was bemoaned, perhaps exaggeratedly, as the premature loss of a potentially major talent. Millais, no less, praised him as "the greatest artist of the century". Other honorary Cliquists included George du Maurier (who seems to have been welcome everywhere) and the Scot John Pettie (1839-93). Pettie's pupil Briton Riviere (1840-1920), who lived at a house called 'Floxley'at 82 Finchley Road, worked up a highly profitable line in slightly daft pictures of dogs, which appealed immensely to sentimental pet lovers. Eyre Crowe (1824-1910), a pupil of Delaroche, painted both historical scenes and social comment and was elected ARA in 1875. He also worked as secretary to the novelist Thackeray.

Death and dispersal broke up the Clique after some fifteen years. Wynfield died of tuberculosis at his house in Grove End Road in May 1877. Leslie migrated to Wallingford, Hodgson to Amersham, Storey to Hampstead, Yeames to Ealing and Calderon to Royal Academy lodgings in Burlington House, leaving Stacy Marks, at 17 Hamilton Terrace, as the sole remaining resident in St John's Wood, where he died in 1898. Hillier's epitaph for the Clique was crisp and crushing. They "interest us not as artists but as an artist community ... The Clique has proved the aptness of its own emblem. Its artists are still on the grill." That was written in 1964. Twenty years later art historian Ann Saunders observed that "their work is, slowly, once again beginning to be appreciated and brought out from the store-rooms of art galleries; another decade may well see a revival ....". Perhaps they may prove to have been prophets not without honour, save in their own country. In 1897 the wealthy German art dealer G.C. Schwabe, who often entertained the group at his home, Yewdon Manor, near Henley-on-Thames, bequeathed to the Hamburg Museum a major collection of their work. When a professional art-dealer collects pictures for his personal pleasure it surely constitutes some sort of endorsement.

Masters of Stone and Bronze

Throughout Victoria's reign sculpture flourished in Britain as never before, benefiting, as a public art form, from the urge to embellish churches and public buildings and to commemorate or celebrate imperial expansion, royal fecundity, civic dignity and foreign victories.

Robert Jackson, who exhibited at the Royal Academy between 1851 and 1878, lived on Maida Hill and Maida Vale for over a quarter of a century. He was long employed on the statuary adorning the new Houses of Parliament and also produced a bust of Irving and carved the statue of buoyant, boyish, belligerent Lord Palmerston which stands in Westminster Abbey's 'Statesman's Aisle'.

John Adams Acton (1830-1910) lived at 17 Abbey Road and 8 (now 14) Langford Place and in 1875 was married at St Mark's, Hamilton Terrace. Between 1854 and 1892 he exhibited 138 pieces at the Royal Academy. His work included busts of the painters Landseer and Frith and the statue of John Wesley which stands outside Wesley's City Road chapel.

The works of **Sir Thomas Brock** (1847-1922) are to be seen prominently throughout the capital. Statues of Robert Raikes, founder of the Sunday School movement, and of Sir Bartle Frere, colonial administrator, stand amid stately shrubbery in Victoria Embankment Gardens; actor Sir Henry Irving gesticulates meaningfully outside the National Portrait Gallery; Captain Cook can now peer no farther than Admiralty Arch from his vantage-point in the Mall, while Lord Lister, pioneer of antiseptics, casts a clinical eye down Portland Place and painter Sir John Millais cheerily acknowledges visitors entering the Tate Gallery. Born in Worcester, Brock learned design at the Royal Worcester Porcelain Factory before coming to London at 19 and apprenticing himself to John Foley, whose studio he took over when Foley died. Brock's first major task was to cast the unfinished statue of the Prince Consort for the Albert Memorial. Brock was also entrusted with designing the elaborate sarcophagus which honours Lord Leighton in St Paul's Cathedral and was himself honoured by being elected first President of the Royal Society of British Sculptors. His masterpiece, or at least his greatest work – all 2,300 tons of it – is the memorial to Queen Victoria in front of Buckingham Palace, which gained him a knighthood. The verdict of the *Dictionary of National Biography* on Brock's prolific output is, however, crushingly dismissive – "an artist of no great originality or inspiration ... the English representative of the more conservative aspects of French sculpture."

Harry Bates (1850-99) served a very practical apprenticeship carving church ornaments before being briefly taught by the hugely influential French master Jules Dalou. Passing through the Royal Academy Schools to win both a gold medal and a travelling studentship, he studied in Paris under Rodin who, surprisingly, made less impact on him than Dalou had in a mere three months. Bates specialised in classical subjects but his most prominent London work is the statue of Earl Roberts on Horseguards' Parade. Actually this is a smaller replica of the original, erected in Calcutta, the year before Bates's death in his studio at 10 Hall Road.

Bates's work in hand was taken over by a contemporary and near neighbour, **Edward Onslow Ford** (1852-1901) of 62 Acacia Road. It was to prove a fatal legacy. Ford had studied in Antwerp and Munich and gained public attention with his statue of Rowland Hill, founder of the penny post. This originally (1882) stood outside the Royal Exchange but was moved to its present site, King

138. Memorial to Onslow Ford at the junction of Grove End Road and Abbey Road. His portrait is on the obverse side.

Edward Street, outside the General Post Office, in 1923. Ford's other important commissions included a portrayal of General Gordon on a camel, the memorial to the poet Shelley at University College, Oxford and portrait heads of such St John's Wood luminaries as Huxley, Spencer, Briton Riviere and Alma-Tadema. Elected RA in 1895, Ford found the additional burden of Bates's uncompleted work too much to deal with and likewise died in his 49th year. Ford's pupil, **Charles Hartwell** (1873-1951), sculpted the St George and the Dragon First World War Memorial outside St John's Wood Church.

The most famous work of **Sir George Frampton** (1860-1928) is undoubtedly Peter Pan in Kensington Gardens. The character was invented by J.M. Barrie for the amusement of the four Llewellyn-Davies boys who were the grandsons of George du Maurier. Trained at the R.A. and in Paris, Frampton was also responsible for the statue of educationist Quintin Hogg in Langham Place, the imposing monument to nurse Edith Cavell in St. Martin's Lane and the rather more modest memorials to journalist W.T. Stead and lyricist W.S. Gilbert on the wall of the Victoria Embankment. Frampton's home and studio were at 32 Queen's Grove from 1894 until 1908, the year in which he was knighted – an experience sufficiently elevating to inspire him to move to 90 (now 92/6) Carlton Hill. A fine portrait of the sculptor, painted by his son Meredith, was acquired by the National Portrait Gallery in 1998.

At the age of 29 **William Goscombe John** (1860-1953) won the Royal Academy's Gold Medal for a bronze he made for Alma-Tadema. John, who was much influenced by the work of Brock and Gilbert, settled in St John's Wood in 1892 and lived there for the rest of his very long life, at 2 Woronzow Studios from 1894-1903, and then at 24 (now 76a) Greville Road. His work, which can be found in cities ranging from his native Cardiff to Calcutta and Cape Town, included a bust of Sir Edmund Gosse and the lively statue of Lord Wolseley on Horse Guards Parade.

Albert Arthur Toft (1862-1949), who lived on Clifton Hill, began his career as an apprentice in the Wedgwood pottery. His work included a medallion portrait of Irving, a statue of his fellow sculptor Gilbert and the striking war memorial to the Royal Fusiliers at Holborn.

Sir (Edgar) Bertram Mackennal (1863-1931) was born in Melbourne, where he trained initially under his father, a Scottish mason specialising in architectural carving. After returning to Europe to study at the Royal Academy and in Paris, Mackennal made England his home, returning to Australia only twice, in 1901 and 1926. His career was crowned with royal favour and public honours. In 1910 he was invited to design George V's coronation medal and coinage. He was also responsible for the equestrian statue of Edward VII which stands in Waterloo Place, outside the Athenaeum and, very appropriately, for the dramatic quadriga *The Horses of the Sun* which surmounts Australia House at Aldwych. In 1922 Mackennal became the first foreign-born artist to be elected as a Royal Academician and subsequently became the first Australian artist to be knighted. He lived at 87a Clifton Hill and later at 38 Marlborough Hill and is commemorated in the name of Mackennal Street, originally called Frederick Street.

Glaswegian **Sir William Reid Dick** (1878-1961) lived in Grove End Road from 1907 to 1938 and then, until his death, at 16 Maida Vale, the former studio of Sir Alfred Gilbert. His major commissions included the fine Pieta and recumbent figure which are the focal points of the memorial chapel honouring Lord Kitchener in St Paul's Cathedral; the Royal Air Force monument which dominates the Embankment at Westminster; the statues of Franklin D. Roosevelt in Grosvenor Square and of George V beside Westminster Abbey; and the emblematic 'Herald' above the entrance to Reuter's News Agency in Fleet Street. Elected RA in 1928, Reid Dick, described by the *Dictionary of National Biography* as "dynamic in spirit and convivial in nature" served as President of the Royal Society of British Sculptors from 1933 to 1938.

A SCULPTOR'S SAGA

The long and troubled career of **Sir Alfred Gilbert** (1854-1934) illustrates dramatically the triumphs, temptations and tragedies attendant on an artistic career. His mother was a professional singer and his father a music teacher who also served as the organist of St Mark's, Hamilton Terrace. The happiest years of Gilbert's childhood were passed at The Woodlands, 89 Maida Vale. Having failed the scholarship examination for the Middlesex Hospital, Gilbert enrolled with relief in Heatherley's Art School at 79 Newman Street, where his fellow pupils included William Rossetti and George Du Maurier. From there he graduated to the RA Schools, where he found the teaching 'beneath contempt', gaining his real training in the studio of J.E. Boehm, a sophisticated Austrian, much favoured by royalty. Gilbert's life then took a suitably Bohemian turn when he secretly married his pregnant cousin Alice at St Saviour's, Paddington and fled incognito to Paris. From 1876 to 1878 he studied at the École des Beaux-Arts, then moved on to Rome where he was fortunate to gain the notice and patronage of the

139. Sir Alfred Gilbert.

ceramics tycoon Henry Doulton and the President of the Royal Academy, Lord Leighton. In 1882 Gilbert's bronze *Perseus Arming* and marble *Kiss of Victory* were exhibited in London to acclaim, marking him out immediately as a coming man.

Returning to London in 1885, Gilbert took a studio in a complex at 76 Fulham Road and soon showed himself a master of the 'lost wax' process of casting, then unknown in England, which he had learned in Italy. He also took a keen interest in Japanese techniques of patination, which enabled him to give unusually brilliant jewel-like finishes to his creations. Gilbert's Westminster Abbey memorial to blind MP Henry Fawcett got him elected ARA in 1887 and, with Leighton's encouragement, the work then poured in – not just statuary, but designing jewellery and even advising on interior decor.

Gilbert was ill-equipped to cope with success. Too ambitious to refuse a commission, especially a technically challenging one, he was also a perfectionist and a procrastinator who would keep clients – even royal clients – dangling for years. Rightly confident of his own abilities, he was sometimes dismissive of professional colleagues, quarrelling with Brock and regarding Onslow Ford, who admired his work, as little more than a plagiarizer. Flattered by invitations to serve on various RA committees, Gilbert devoted long hours to administration and even longer hours to the company of new-found friends at the Garrick Club. He was now on familiar terms with Henry James, Millais, Lord Rothschild and even Princess Louise, daughter of Queen Victoria. Louise was herself a sculptor and the secret lover of Gilbert's old mentor Boehm – whose unfinished commissions he took over after Boehm's sudden death (in the arms of Princess Louise). Hopeless with managing his time, Gilbert was even worse when it came to money. But it was some years before the crash came.

Gilbert's greatest projects were elaborate monuments to the Duke of Clarence, heir presumptive to the future Edward VII, at Windsor, and to Lord Shaftesbury, the social reformer, at Piccadilly Circus. The latter, which became known as Eros, pioneered the use of aluminium in statuary. Typically there was no formal contract and constant changes to the design greatly added to the costs Gilbert was obliged to bear. He eventually lost £4,000. Public reactions were mixed. Gilbert himself cavilled at its location - "an impossible site on which to place any outcome of the human brain except possibly an underground lavatory."

As if to guarantee his own destruction, Gilbert borrowed £7,500 to build himself a massive studio complex and family home at 16 Maida Vale. His annual studio expenses alone would run to £1,200 a year. Arranged around a courtyard, the building boasted both a huge ground floor general studio and a private upper studio, which was itself large enough to have a stage for family theatricals and meetings of the Madrigal Society. In the grounds Gilbert hosted sessions for a fencing-club whose members included Alma-Tadema.

On 10 March 1893 Queen Victoria herself visited Gilbert in his studio and in 1897 elevated him to membership of the newly created Royal Victorian Order, which had been established to reward personal service to the sovereign. In retrospect Gilbert was to concede that these were the years of hubris - "The new home and studio I built in Maida Vale was the scene of the commencement of a life as new and on a scale commensurate with the vastness of my folly in burdening myself with such a shell ... The very walls and beams at times seemed to be closing in and ready to crush me."

He began to experience professional reverses. His statue of the politician John Bright was so much disliked that it was ignominiously withdrawn from the House of Commons. He failed to win the appointment as Principal of the Royal College of Art, which he craved in hopes of a steady income. As disappointed clients and discontented creditors circled around, he withdrew into his Maida Vale 'Fortress', avoiding unpleasant encounters. His final fling was a lavish wedding reception for one of his children, with two hun-

140. The studio at 4 Greville Place, of sculptor, Gilbert Bayes (1872-1952), who became President of the Royal Society of British Sculptors. His most prominent London work is the great clock on the front of Selfridge's, Oxford Street.

dred guests and catering by Whiteley's – whose bill remained unpaid. Soon afterwards the gas and water were cut off. Then came expulsion from the Garrick for non-payment of his subscription. The contents of 16 Maida Vale were auctioned off for a mere £450. Following a formal declaration of bankruptcy and an orgy of smashing plaster models to prevent unauthorised castings, Gilbert in 1902 migrated to Bruges for the next quarter century. 16 Maida Vale was bought by another St John's Wood sculptor, Herbert Hampton.

While offering far fewer temptations than London, Bruges failed to force Gilbert into stability. He took a large, fifteenth-century house, not dissimilar to 16 Maida Vale and within months was begging friends for loans. Kindly Queen Alexandra sent him £100. There were allegations of alcoholism and even morphine addiction as explanations of Gilbert's continuing failure to complete such commissions as he could still get. He continued to refuse to open letters, to the dismay of his dwindling circle of supporters. In 1904 his long-suffering wife, Alice, finally left

him. *Truth* magazine ran a devastating expose which rubbished his remaining reputation and led him to resign his MRVO and membership of the Royal Academy. Too poor to pay even for his mother's burial plot, Gilbert took refuge in endless work, but to little financial purpose, and sought consolation with a Flemish widow – who brought seven children with her. Gilbert and his new family survived the German war-time occupation of Bruges, despite being reduced to living on pears from their orchard. But, professionally discredited, he even missed out on the massive demand for memorials which followed the ending of the conflict. Longing to return to Britain, Gilbert found himself, in his seventies, tied to a wife who had never left Bruges, could speak only Flemish and was totally unable to cope with any other way of life. Their separation was the price of Gilbert's rehabilitation; it came in the form of a Civil List pension and – almost incredibly – a royal commission for a monument to Queen Alexandra. Gilbert's 'Swan Song' won him re-election to the Royal Academy and a knighthood.

The Theatricals

One of the more remarkable cultural transformations of the nineteenth century was the rise to respectability of the theatrical profession – or at least of some of its leading members. That the profession had finally 'arrived' was signified unambiguously in 1895 by the knighting of Sir Henry Irving (1838-1905), the first thespian to be thus honoured. Although he was never a resident of St John's Wood, Irving decisively affected the careers of many of the theatricals who were.

THE MANAGERS

George Colman the Younger (1762-1836) was the son of a dramatist and friend of Garrick and Goldsmith. His father's best play was *The Clandestine Marriage* (1766) – which is just what George the Younger embarked on at the age of twenty-two. In 1794 he succeeded his father as manager of Covent Garden. Talented enough as both actor and dramatist, he was far less stable as a character,

being both extravagant and reckless in seeking expensive lawsuits. In 1811 he was living at 4 Melina Place and in 1824 he moved into 5 Melina Place, the same year as he became Examiner of Plays, in which capacity he was to exhibit a prudery which might be considered mildly surprising in the light of his own domestic arrangements and past performances in broad comedy.

John Laurence Toole (1820-96), some time resident of 44 Maida Vale, did not make his first professional stage appearance, in Dublin, until he was thirty-two. Provincial touring was followed by a London debut in 1856 in Charles Webb's *Belphegor the Mountebank*, Marie Wilton, the future Lady Bancroft, making her debut in the same production. Soon afterwards Toole played alongside Irving, who was to remain a life-long friend. In 1858 he was recommended by Dickens to Ben Webster at the Adelphi, his theatrical home until 1869, when he became a partner in the management of the Gaiety with **John Hollingshead** (1827-1904), who lived at 14 North Bank. Hollingshead came late to theatrical management, having been on the staff of *Household Words* and worked as a

141. John Laurence Toole.

142. John Hollingshead.

143. Sir Squire Bancroft, monocled and with manners to match..

freelance contributor to *Punch* and the *Cornhill Magazine*. Burlesque was their standard stock in trade, many of the scripts being supplied by **Robert Reece** (1838-1891), who lived at 58 Adelaide Road. Trained as a lawyer, Reece escaped the civil service by reworking such familiar fare as the stories of Robin Hood, Aladdin and Dick Whittington. At the Gaiety, the first London establishment to combine a theatre, restaurant and bar in a single building, Hollingshead pioneered the novel notion of matinée performances, experimented with external electric lighting and staged London's first performance of a play by Ibsen. Hollingshead believed in paying well and getting the best, his employees including the 'divine' Sarah Bernhardt (1844-1923), who on one of her sojourns in London lived at 14 Alpha Road. Having amassed a considerable fortune he lost it all speculating in provincial theatres. Hollingshead was to be buried near the equally extravagant Augustus Harris (*see* below).

Toole eventually parted from Hollingshead to take over the Charing Cross Theatre in William IV Street, reopening it in 1882 as Toole's, the first London theatre to be named after its proprietor. Here Toole maintained his commitment to innovation by staging J.M. Barrie's first play in 1892. In his mid-seventies and crippled by gout, Toole was finally forced to close his doors in 1895 and quit St John's Wood for Brighton, where he died

a decade later.

Charles Wyndham (actually Culverwell) (1837-1919) had an unusual apprenticeship for theatrical management, having served as an army surgeon in the American civil war. A specialist in light comedy, Wyndham was also known for his name role in *David Garrick*. Wyndham took over the newly-built Criterion Theatre at Piccadilly in 1876 and built Wyndham's in Charing Cross Road in 1899. In 1903 he staged the first English performance of Rostand's *Cyrano de Bergerac*. Wyndham lived at Boscombe Lodge, Finchley Road and was knighted in 1892.

Sir Squire Bancroft (1841-1926) came from an entirely untheatrical background and worked his way up from repertory in Birmingham. Having married former child-star and actress Marie Wilton (1839-1921) in 1867, he found success by staging stylish drawing-room comedies and using his knowledge of stagecraft to develop more practical scenery. He also did much to raise the standing of the acting profession – not least by paying his actors well. Invariably monocled, and with manners to match, Bancroft was rich enough to retire from the boards at 44 and devote many years to producing volumes of largely repetitive memoirs. The Bancrofts lived at 11 Grove End Road before they became rich and famous and moved to Cavendish Square.

The portentously named **Sir Augustus Henry Glossop Harris** (1852-96) lived at The Elms, Avenue Road. As a boy Harris played under Wyndham's direction at the Criterion, then toured with Mapleson (*see* p.90) as a stage manager. He took over the management of the Theatre Royal, Drury Lane when he was just 27 and held the position until his early death at 44. The son of the manager of Covent Garden, Harris became so closely identified with his office that he was nicknamed 'Augustus Druriolanus'. Imitating the professional predilections of his father, Harris concentrated on producing spectacular melodramas and lavish Christmas shows, renowned for their magnificent scenery and ingenious stage machinery. Even in presenting traditional pantomimes he innovated by interpolating music hall turns, such as acrobats, clowns and knockabout comedians. The critic Klein found Harris "the strangest imaginable mixture of conceit and modesty, rashness and discretion, extravagance and common sense" but was greatly impressed by his remarkable energy and powers of organisation and not least by his ability to seek out and benefit from technical advice. On one occasion Klein witnessed the meticulous rehearsal of a spectacularly spine-chilling scene involving spear-wielding warriors choreographed according to the

144. Augustus Harris.

instructions of one Major Kitchener – the future icon of Great War recruiting posters. Harris's career was crowned with election to the office of Sheriff of the City of London and a knighthood. A bust of appropriately imperial pompousness preserves his memory outside his theatre to this day.

Sir George Alexander (1858-1918) served his apprenticeship under Irving between 1881 and 1889 before taking on the St James's Theatre, where he proclaimed a policy of supporting new British authors and found early triumphs with Oscar Wilde's *Lady Windermere's Fan* (1892) and Pinero's *The Second Mrs. Tanqueray* (1893). In 1895 he pioneered the role of Jack Worthing in the first production of *The Importance of Being Earnest* and in 1896 the dual role of Rudolf Rassendyll and the King in Anthony Hope's *The Prisoner of Zenda*. Alexander's policy of patronising new talent was tempered by a cold commercial caution. When

Wilde was disgraced he kept *Earnest* running – but removed the author's name from the playbills. (He did, however, honourably forward royalties to Wilde during and after his imprisonment and later secured the performing rights to *Earnest* for the benefit of Wilde's children.) Alexander, sometime a St John's Wood resident, was not, moreover, afraid to court controversy and on one occasion found himself in court for his gallantry in defending a prostitute from police harassment. As an employer he was good to his company and they were loyal to him.

Matheson Lang (1879-1948), who had a house in Avenue Road, toured the Empire indefatigably in his youth, most notably in the name part of *Mr. Wu*, an Anglo-Chinese melodrama. In 1914 he inaugurated the Old Vic's long association with Shakespeare. **Sir Cedric Hardwicke** (1893-1964), a neighbour in Avenue Road, initially built his career on playing Shaw but after 1939 settled in New York.

Bernard Miles (1907-91) served a lengthy apprenticeship in repertory before founding the Mermaid Theatre in 1951, initially in a former school hall in the grounds of his St John's Wood home at 43 Acacia Road. In 1959 the Mermaid found a permanent, purpose-built home at Puddle Dock, Blackfriars in the City of London. The Mermaid's founder was knighted in 1969 and eventually honoured with a Life Peerage. Millions who never went near a theatre nevertheless had a great affection for the rich, gravelly voice of a hundred whimsical radio monologues of rural life and heeded his voice-over to the advertisement urging the British to 'Go To Work on an Egg '.

THE ACTORS

Character specialist **Daniel Terry** (1789-1829) was a friend of Sir Walter Scott, several of whose novels he adapted for the stage. He made his London debut in Colman's *The Clandestine Marriage*. Having played extensively at Covent Garden, supported Sarah Siddons in her farewell performance and appeared at Drury Lane, he made a brief but unsuccessful excursion into management at the Adelphi but soon retired. He was buried in the churchyard of St.John's Wood Chapel.

Charles Albert Fechter (1824-79) – 'the Hamlet of the blond wig' – lived at 11 Marlborough Place and 30 Park Road. He had a German father and an English mother but spoke French as his first language, playing in French as well as English (with a marked French accent). He made his debut with the Comedie Française at sixteen and was the first to play Armand Duval in Dumas' *The Lady of the Camelias* in 1852. The critic G.H. Lewes, a singularly unhandsome man himself, paid tribute to Fechter's striking looks but there was more to him than exceptional stage presence. Fechter's subtle but passionate interpretation of *Hamlet* in 1861 came as a revelation to fellow professionals, confirmed his English reputation and encouraged him to take over management of the Lyceum, where he effected a 'mechanical revolution' by installing lifts and grooved machinery which could change whole sets at unprecedented speed. From 1869 onwards he enjoyed further triumphs in New York. Possessing what his friend and admirer Dickens called "a perfect genius for quarrelling", Fechter made numerous professional enemies and further complicated his career with excessive drinking and bigamy. In 1876 he retired to the obscurity of a farm, dying, ironically, in Quakertown.

Genevieve Teresa ('Lucy') Ward (1838-1922) was the first actress to be created DBE, in 1921. Born in New York, she initially sang opera as the improbably named Madame Ginevra Guerrabella. Illness and overwork destroyed her singing voice, forcing her to make her stage debut in Manchester in 1873, as Lady Macbeth, a role she was later to play successfully in French. The last phase of her full-time career, from 1891 to 1900, was spent with Irving's company, but she continued to make occasional appearances until her eighty-second year. In 1913 she was living in Avenue Road.

Wilson Barrett (1846-1904), who took over George Eliot's house at 21 North Bank, was a melodrama specialist who "lacked only height to make him a fine figure of a man" and wasted his undoubted abilities on inferior material, most of which he wrote for himself. His career was made, and in a sense blighted, by his own play *The Sign of the Cross*, in which he played Marcus Superbus to such acclaim and financial success that he was unable to escape the part thereafter. Dealing with the theme of conversion, this "melodrama of frantic spirituality" became the subject of earnest sermons and was said to have attracted to the theatre thousands who would otherwise never have crossed its threshold.

William Charles Terriss (1847-97) was actually born in Circus Road. Following a disastrous debut in Birmingham in 1867, he tried his hand as a merchant seaman and a tea-planter in Assam before settling in the Falkland Islands as a sheep-farmer. His daughter, Ellaline (1871-1971), who was to follow her own hugely successful stage career and marry actor-manager Sir Seymour Hicks, was born during this interval of exile. Returning to the stage in 1873, Terriss, like so many talents of the day, was drawn into Irving's company from 1880 to 1885. From there he went to the Adelphi where

his muscular talent for swashbuckling hero parts won him the punning sobriquet 'No. 1 Adelphi Terriss'. Otherwise known as 'Breezy Bill ' from his upbeat, outgoing manner Terriss was brutally stabbed to death at the Adelphi stage-door by a deranged actor with a personal grudge against him. Terriss's untimely death cost the profession, in the title of the play he had staged in 1895 with the young Seymour Hicks "One of the Best".

Edward Smith Willard (1853-1915) of Blenheim Road was renowned for his villain roles in popular melodrama. In 1889 he took over management of the Shaftesbury and later toured North America. During the course of the latter Willard appeared with the American actress Maxine Elliott (1868-1940). More famed for beauty than talent, she acted for money and abandoned the boards as soon as she had accumulated a fortune, much of which derived from gifts and financial tips from numerous admirers, including King Edward VII. She made her London debut in 1895 at Daly's in *Two Gentlemen of Verona*. In 1900 her sister, also an actress, married Johnston Forbes-Robertson. Having settled at 20 Abbey Road, when the Great War broke out Elliott threw herself into war work to such an extent that in 1920 she had to return to the American stage to repair her finances.

Eugene Stratton (1861-1918) was an American 'black-face' impersonator, who came to London with the Haverly Minstrels in 1880. When the minstrel craze passed, he switched to music hall but had no success until he reverted to his negro persona as a solo artist. In this guise Stratton was without rivals until his retirement in 1914. Whistling soulfully, soft-shoe shuffling on a darkened stage, he imbued a racial caricature with dignity and elegance and made 'Lily of Laguna' a musical 'standard'. He lived at 59 Wellington Road.

John Martin-Harvey (1863-1944) made his debut in 1881 and joined Irving the following year to become first his understudy and, latterly, for many critics, his professional descendant. In 1899 he played Sydney Carton in his own dramatic adaptation of *A Tale of Two Cities* with such success that he was compelled to repeat it throughout his subsequent career. In 1912, when he was living at 30 Avenue Road, he gave the performance of his life in *Oedipus* and latterly added Shaw to his repertoire. But, more interested in the theatre than drama, he was quite willing to countenance playing histrionic hokum if it made the box office bulge and accumulated a comfortable fortune touring the provinces and Canada. In 1889 he married Angelita Helena Margarita de Silva Ferro (1869-1949) who, as Nina de Silva, was his stage partner for decades - and unfortunately not nearly as good as he thought she was. He was knighted in 1921.

The family background of Mary Susan Etherington was obscured by her own fanciful elaborations connecting her in various ways with shadowy Guards officers, courtiers and the Gladstone family. A standard biographical work records delicately that "the details of her early life are not well authenticated". What is certain is that, despite greeting the world in the Marylebone Road premises of a dipsomaniac stationer, she received an expensive education at a Belgian convent, in Paris and at the Royal Academy of Music, where she won bronze, silver and gold medals. Nature made her petite but gave her beautiful, expressive hands, a stunning figure and a fine soprano voice. She had instinctive good taste in dress and a polished curtsy which became "almost world-renowned". As **Marie Tempest** (1864 -1942) she would conquer her chosen profession in whatever she attempted. Following her debut in 1885, she reigned supreme in New York from 1890 to 1895, then returned to star in a string of musical comedies at Daly's for the following five years. In 1901 she switched to straight comedy, taking the name part in *Becky Sharp*, an adaptation of Thackeray's *Vanity Fair*. Her success, however, reflected true dedication to her craft. Temperate in her life-style, she avoided late parties and never grudged long

145. Marie Tempest.

hours in rehearsal. Moving on from comedy, she played leading roles in works by contemporary writers and toured the world, playing as far away as China and Japan. Her testimonial matinee, staged at Drury Lane to mark her half century on the stage, was played in the presence of King George V and Queen Mary, raising £5,000 which went to found a Marie Tempest Ward for the benefit of actors and actresses at St George's Hospital, Hyde Park Corner. Marie Tempest found her true happiness with her third husband, the actor William Graham Browne, an Ulsterman who became her most effective director.

George Arliss (1868-1946) came to prominence playing opposite Mrs Patrick Campbell in *The Second Mrs Tanqueray* and acquired a lifelong personal asset by playing the name part in *Disraeli*, a play written specifically for him in 1911. After some twenty years in the USA (where the American Academy of Arts and Letters awarded him a Gold Medal for diction), Arliss returned to London, settling at No. 1 Clifton Villas. During the second part of his career he attained even greater fame as a film actor in a series of historical biopics. A master of understatement on stage and screen, in private life Arliss also lived undemonstratively. A committed vegetarian, he was also a demon at contract bridge.

George Robey (actually Wade) (1869-1954), although usually associated with music hall songs and skits, was sufficiently versatile to play Falstaff, star in revue in the 'Bing Boys' shows and manage the Prince's Theatre. The son of a peripatetic civil engineer, he became a fluent speaker of German and attended Leipzig University, where he was wounded in one of the ritualised duels organised by student fraternities. Changing his name to avoid embarrassment to his family, Robey made his first music hall appearance at twenty-one and rapidly proved himself a master of large and unruly audiences, less the 'Prime Minister of Mirth' than the tyrant of crushing repartee. The greatest tribute to his mastery of stagecraft was that he attracted a cult following among serious theatre critics. He was also a talented amateur painter, a gifted writer, a competent cricketer, a keen collector of porcelain and postage stamps, a maker of violins and a knowledgeable student of Egyptology. Robey was offered a knighthood for his services to charity after the First World War but thought the honour too great for a comedian and accepted a CBE instead. After a lifetime of service to both the theatre and charity he was finally knighted in 1954. In 1908 Robey was living at 35 Circus Road and in 1924 at 70 Finchley Road.

146. George Robey.

DRAMATISTS

George R. Sims (1847-1922), a resident of Hamilton Terrace, was a one-man script factory whose largely ephemeral output ranged over melodrama, farce and burlesque. Many of his efforts, such as *The Lights o' London* (1881) were set against the background of the capital. The recreations which occupied his off-duty hours he listed as " battledore and shuttlecock, bull-dogs and motoring ".

Sir Arthur Wing Pinero (1855-1934) began as a 'utility' actor before working as a member of Irving's Lyceum troupe from 1876 to 1881, where he excelled in what Ellen Terry called 'silly ass'

roles. Already, however, he had turned to writing. *Two Hundred a Year*, the first of fifty-four plays, was staged in 1877. By 1881 *English Dramatists of Today* hailed him as a promising dramatic talent and by 1885, when he already had fifteen plays to his credit, he was able to give up acting altogether. His 1888 play *Sweet Lavender* ran for 684 performances at Terry's. While maintaining his output of similar lightweight confections, he then developed a parallel stream of 'problem plays', which managed to examine conventional morality without exactly crossing the line of good taste by challenging it. *The Second Mrs. Tanqueray* (1893) explored the dilemmas of a 'woman with a past' - a very St John's Wood sort of theme – and made Mrs Patrick Campbell a household name. In 1896 Pinero was living at 62 Hamilton Terrace.

Herbert Farjeon (1887-1945) excelled in writing and directing witty sketches, performed mainly in the suitably intimate setting of the Little Theatre. Scholarly in disposition, Farjeon at different times edited both the *Shakespeare Journal* and the definitive *Nonesuch* editions of Shakespeare's plays. He lived at 34 Loudoun Road.

Christopher Fry (1907-) worked as a schoolmaster, actor and theatre director before making his name in the 1940s with a series of verse plays on mystical and religious themes, which were compared with the work of T.S. Eliot. Financial success, however, came from his exuberantly verbal comedies, such as *The Lady's Not for Burning* (1949). Fry, who lived at 37 Blomfield Road in the 1950s and 1960s, also made successful translations of plays by Anouilh and Giraudoux.

A UNIQUE TALENT

The achievements of the acrobat and tightrope-walker known as **Blondin** (1824-1897) were undeniably dramatic. Born Jean-Francois Gravelet, he gave his first public performance at six, billed as 'The Little Wonder '. In 1859 he crossed the Niagara Falls on a tightrope – then did it again blindfold, and again pushing a wheelbarrow, then again with a man on his back. In 1860 he crossed Niagara on stilts and three hundred more times, weighed down with various other impedimenta. In 1861 he gave his first performance in London, at the Crystal Palace, turning somersaults, *on stilts*, on a tightrope a hundred and seventy feet up in the air! At sixty-five he performed on the high wire in New York, where he rode on it on a bicycle and also balanced a stove on it to cook omelettes for his spellbound audience. He made his last public appearance at the age of seventy-two.

He lived at Niagara Villa, later re-named Moore House, Finchley Road, then at 6 Boscobel Place, destroyed by the Grand Central Railway.

Men of Enterprise

MUNITIONS AND MISERLINESS

The curious career of munitions millionaire **John Farquhar** (1751-1826) began in poverty in Aberdeenshire and ended in miserly squalor in Park Road, St John's Wood. Originally intending a military career in India, he was lamed for life by a hip wound and obliged to turn to commerce. An enthusiastic amateur chemist, Farquhar was consulted by the Governor-General of Bengal about the organisation of a gunpowder factory and ended up running it. Eventually he became sole contractor of munitions for the British authorities in India, accumulating a personal fortune of half a million pounds in the process. Returning to England, he was to triple that sum before his death. Although frequently generous to charities and capriciously moved to purchase the great Gothic folly of Fonthill Abbey for £330,000, Farquhar habitually lived with a frugality bordering on privation, attended by a single old woman and subsisting on little more than rice and bread. Courteous and cultured despite his slovenly appearance and bizarre behaviour, Farquhar died intestate. His fortune was divided equally between the seven nephews and nieces who dutifully came to see him interred at St John's Wood Chapel.

GENIUS OF THE KITCHEN

For a time one of the most celebrated of chefs lived in St John's Wood. **Alexis Soyer** (1809-1858) was apprenticed to his vocation at twelve and ended his teenage years as head chef, with a staff of twelve, at Grignon's a noted restaurant in the Boulevard des Italiens in Paris. But he fled the disorders accompanying the revolution of 1830 to join his brother in London in the kitchens of the Duke of Cambridge. A succession of aristocratic employments followed over the next half dozen years, culminating in appointment as chef to the prestigious Reform Club in 1837. Soyer's phenomenal powers of organisation were convincingly demonstrated on the occasion of Queen Victoria's coronation the following year when he co-ordinated a breakfast for 2,000 members and their guests, off-site, using Gwydyr House in Whitehall as his base. On subsequent occasions he also arranged formal banquets in honour of visiting dignitaries, such as Ibrahim Pasha, naval heroes, like Admiral Sir Charles Napier and the Prime Minister, Lord Palmerston.   In 1841 Soyer pioneered the use of gas in cooking by introducing gas stoves and grills into the kitchens at the Reform.

The scepticism and snobbery of professional colleagues retarded the general adoption of gas in cooking for another thirty years but Soyer was unshaken in his belief that this technological advance represented 'the greatest comfort ever introduced into any culinary arrangement' and his Pall Mall kitchens even became a considerable tourist attraction.

In 1847 Soyer displayed the social conscience which was one of his most attractive characteristics by setting up soup kitchens in Dublin during the catastrophic Irish famine and writing *"Soyer's Charitable Cookery, or The Poor Man's Regenerator"*. In 1849 he invented a modestly-named 'magic stove' which could be used for cooking at the table itself. Sales of this device, plus his salary at the Reform, brought him in an income of over £1,000 a year. But he was soon to over-stretch himself disastrously. In 1851 Soyer tried to take advantage of the crowds anticipated to attend the Great Exhibition of Arts and Industry by opening a restaurant, *Soyer's Symposium*, in Gore House, former home of the Countess of Blessington, which stood, where the Albert Hall now stands, right opposite the Exhibition site. Despite a triumphant opening, orchestrated by one of its key backers, the haughty, hedonistic journalist George Augustus Sala, the venture proved disastrous as the costs of a lavish refurbishment and sloppy management resulted in a loss of £7,000.

Undaunted by this setback, Soyer in 1855 volunteered himself, at his own expense, to join Miss Nightingale in Turkey, where he speedily established efficient and wholesome catering arrangements for the British wounded of the Crimean war. In the course of this remarkable project Soyer also designed a 'cooking wagon' which established the basic pattern of the British Army field-stove until the Second World War. Apart from several books of recipes for both the affluent – *The Gastronomic Regenerator* – and the impoverished – *A Shilling Cookery* – Soyer also published a history of food – *Pantropheon* – which astonished critics with the depth of the author's learning. Soyer was almost certainly the model for M. Mirobolant in Thackeray's *History of Pendennis*. The great chef's domestic life was saddened by the early death of his talented English wife Emma (1813-42). An actress who also showed prodigious talent as a portraitist while only a child, she exhibited fourteen pictures at the Royal Academy in the course of her brief artistic career. Her sentimental works found great popularity with the early Victorian public, winning her the title of 'the English Murillo' and gaining her a reputation even in France, where her work was known through engravings. In the fifth year of her marriage to Soyer she was so badly

147. *Sir George Gilbert Scott.*

148. *Sir Joseph and Lady Bazalgette .*

terrified by a thunderstorm of exceptional ferocity that she went into premature labour and died. The stricken Soyer erected a sumptuous monument in her memory at Kensal Green cemetery. In 1848 he exhibited 140 of her pictures as 'Soyer's Philanthropic Gallery' to raise money in support of a soup kitchen he was sponsoring in Spitalfields. He, too, lies at Kensal Green, having died after a short illness at his home, 15 Marlborough Road.

CAPITAL CHARACTERS

Few men have had a more decisive impact on the face of London than **Sir George Gilbert Scott** (1811-1878), who lived at 23 (then 12) Avenue Road. Indeed, the wonder is that he had time to live anywhere at all. A disciple of Pugin and fervent proponent of High Gothic, Scott ran the largest architectural practice in Victorian England. His London projects alone include the Albert Memorial, St Pancras Station Hotel, the Foreign Office and at least nineteen churches in the suburbs. He also built some fifty workhouses, as well as Edinburgh's Anglican cathedral, and was also involved in numerous restoration projects. His enthusiastic historicism got the better of him to such an extent that it provoked William Morris to found the Society for the Protection of Ancient Buildings (or 'Anti-Scrape' as he called it privately) to stop Scott putting churches back to the condition which he believed historically 'correct' – even if it corresponded to no actual stage of their past existence.

A modest wall-monument beside the northern end of Hungerford Bridge proclaims of the ferociously bewhiskered **Sir Joseph Bazalgette** (1819-91) *'Flumen Ad Vincula Posuit '* – he put chains on the river. As chief engineer to the Metropolitan Board of Works Bazalgette, who retired to 17 Hamilton Terrace, was responsible for the construction of both 83 miles of London's main drainage system (1858-75) and the Embankment of the River Thames.

Sir George Henry Lewis (1833-1911) was a lawyer who specialized in sleaze and scandal. Equally adept in exposing either or covering them up, he made many friends and not a few enemies in theatrical, artistic, financial and political circles.

Educated at University College School, he qualified as a solicitor and joined the family firm in 1856. Scarcely a *cause célèbre* of the rest of the century did not find him on one side or the other. Meticulous in his preparation, elephantine in memory, brilliant in cross-examination, he was also gifted with an intuition which contemporaries swore would make Sherlock Holmes appear a dullard in comparison. Despite a career which would have entitled him to adopt a world-weary cynicism without affectation, Lewis was an energetic supporter of more liberal divorce laws and of legislation to curb the unscrupulous excesses of usurers. He lived for a time in St John's Wood at an unknown address.

Archaeologist, anthropologist, administrator and author, **Sir Laurence Gomme** (1853-1921) unsurprisingly listed his recreations in *Who's Who* as 'change of work'. In various capacities Gomme worked for the government of London for forty-two years eventually becoming Clerk to the London County Council in 1900. Apart from writing historical novels and *The Making of London* (1911), he was also President of the Folklore Society. Gomme lived at 20 Marlborough Place.

SCIENCE FOR INDUSTRY

Ludwig Mond (1839-1909) founded the firm which, in the 1920s, his son Alfred, Lord Melchett, was to turn into the giant chemicals conglomerate I.C.I. Born in Cassel, Germany, Mond studied at Heidelberg under Rudolf Bunsen (he of the burner) and worked in chemical plants in Germany and the Netherlands before coming to Britain in the 1860s. Mond made his reputation, and a fortune of more than a million pounds, through his development of techniques for the more efficient recovery or manufacture of such basic materials as sulphur, chlorine, nitrogen, ammonia and nickel. Naturalised as a Briton in 1880, Mond settled at The Poplars, 18-20 Avenue Road in 1884, though he spent his winters in Rome. Both locations reflected his keen interest in art, of which he was an enthusiastic and discriminating collector. A self-consciously progressive employer, Mond was one of the pioneers of the eight hour day and provided both model housing and playing-fields for his employees, as well as establishing a trust fund for those who were disabled or elderly.

Sir John Ambrose Fleming (1849-1945), who lived at 9 Clifton Gardens, is specifically remembered as the inventor of the wireless valve but

149. *The dining room of The Poplars in Avenue Road, designed by J.M. Brydon, in 1859. The house was later occupied by Ludwig Mond.*

150. *Design for a house in Avenue Road in 1859, thought to be The Poplars, the later home of Ludwig Mond.*

more broadly could be seen as the father of electrical engineering in Britain. Educated at University College School, Fleming graduated with first class honours from University College, London, despite the fact that for the last two years of his degree course he had only been able to study part time while working full time as a stockbroker's clerk. He then worked as a science teacher at two public schools to save up the money needed to take him on to Cambridge, where he studied under Clerk Maxwell and did research in the Cavendish Laboratories. In 1885 Fleming was appointed to a professorship at University College London, a post he held for the next 41 years. In the course of his long and distinguished career he published over a hundred scientific papers, was instrumental in founding the National Physical Laboratory and worked as a consultant or collaborator with Edison, Marconi and Logie Baird, being thus involved in the origins of electric lighting, radio and television.

Edward Goodrich Acheson (1856-1931) was born in Pennsylvania of Scotch-Irish descent. A self-taught engineer, he took out his first patent, for a rock-boring machine, at seventeen; 68 more were to follow. A draftsman for Edison at the age of 25, Acheson travelled on his behalf throughout Europe in the 1880s, supervising the installation of electric lighting systems. His own major technical achievement was the invention of the artificial industrial abrasive known as carborundum but he also revolutionised the manufacture of graphite and founded no less than five industrial corporations. From 1912 to 1915 Acheson lived in a house on Prince Albert Road (since demolished) overlooking Regent's Park. His many inventions, applicable in such diverse fields as mining, ceramics and electrical engineering, won him honours in Russia and Sweden as well as his native United States.

FATHERS OF THE CINEMA
William Friese-Greene (1855-1921), resident at 136 Maida Vale from 1888 to 1891, played a crucial, if now barely acknowledged, role in the development of cinematography. He successfully made a camera which took a sequence of photographs on a roll of perforated film moving intermittently behind a shutter; but it appears to have taken pictures too slowly to achieve the full illusion of animation. Although Friese-Green may have shot the world's first movie film at his Maida Vale address, he never gave a successful public demonstration of his invention and so credit for the motion picture camera has traditionally been given to Thomas Edison. Friese-Green later conducted

151. No. 136 Maida Vale, the home of cinema pioneer, William Friese-Greene. The house has recently been demolished.

pioneering experiments in stereoscopic and colour cinematography but lacked the technical back-up and financial resources to bring his efforts to fruition.

More famous in the film world was **Sir Alexander Korda** (1893-1956) who lived at 81 Avenue Road from 1933 to 1939. Those were his golden years. Born in Hungary, Korda had already had a cosmopolitan career, producing films in Budapest, Vienna, Berlin, Hollywood and Paris before founding London Film Productions Ltd in 1932. He was the nearest Britain ever had to a Hollywood-style mogul. His first great success came with *The Private Life of Henry VIII* (1933), an over-the-top bawdy romp, which launched the career of Charles Laughton, who won an Oscar in the name part, the first British actor to be so honoured. *Henry VIII* had been shot in five weeks on a budget of £60,000. Its international success enabled Korda to get the financial backing of the mighty Prudential Assurance Company and open his own modern studios at Denham. At 'Hollywood on Thames', he set out to show that his adopted country could turn out films to rival the American product. *Things to Come* (1936), based on H.G.Wells' prophetic novel, proved all too prescient. In 1939 Korda set aside work on his lavish Technicolor fantasy, *The Thief of Baghdad*, to splice together – in a month – the first British propaganda film of the Second World War, *The Lion has Wings*. By so doing Korda convinced his friend Winston Churchill that cinema could make a vital contribution to the war effort and thus saved it from extinction to experience its finest hour. Korda was knighted in 1942, the first film-maker to be so honoured. His post-war successes included the classic Orson Welles mystery *The Third Man* (1949) and Olivier's *Richard III* (1956).

APOSTLE OF ARTS AND CRAFTS

C.F.A. Voysey (1857-1941) was a true architectural innovator who created his own distinctive aesthetic signature. According to the *Dictionary of National Biography* "he deliberately avoided the classical or neo-Georgian fashions which were popular about the turn of the century, regarding them as un-English". All the more surprising then that when it came to his own home he settled for a conventional villa at 6 Carlton Hill. A descendant of John Wesley, whom he is said to have greatly resembled, Voysey was a disciple of William Morris and himself became the mentor of Charles Rennie Mackintosh. Voysey claimed to have taken up architecture because it was a profession which, at that time, required entrants to pass no qualifying examinations. His interests, however, ranged far beyond building as such, leading him to design furniture, wallpaper, fabrics and stained glass. His country houses were typically long and low, with strong horizontal lines, steep, often hipped, slate roofs, roughcast walls, bold buttresses and small, leaded-light windows.

Despite a fall from fashion, Voysey remained true to his principles and in 1924 became master of the Art Workers Guild, which had been founded in the 1880s to perpetuate the ideals of craftsmanship represented by William Morris and his followers. Architectural historian Alastair Service notes that "his influence is seen in almost every London suburb built between 1900 and 1940". Examples of Voysey's work include the studio house at 17 St Dunstan's Road, West Kensington and Annesley Lodge, at the corner of Platt's Lane and Kidderpore Avenue, Hampstead, which he built for his father.

FOUNDERS OF ISRAEL

David Ben-Gurion (1886-1973), first Prime Minister of Israel, was born in Poland but in 1906 emigrated to Palestine, where he worked as a farmer. During the First World War he enlisted in the Jewish Legion against the Ottoman Turks but Allenby's army conquered Palestine before the Legion could reach the battlefield. In 1920 Ben-Gurion founded a workers' federation, the Histadrut, which became in effect the nucleus of the future state of Israel, and in 1930 he launched and led a socialist party, Mapai. Throughout the following years he was at the heart of the struggle to establish an independent state and in 1948 was personally responsible for the declaration of its independence. Ben-Gurion's determination in welding disparate underground forces into a united army enabled the precarious state to preserve its existence against Arab assault. Apart from a brief period (1953-5) he led Israel as prime minister from 1948 to 1963, finally retiring from politics in 1970. A blue plaque marks his modest one time home at 75 Warrington Crescent.

Israel Moses Sieff (1889-1972) met Simon Marks when they were both pupils at Manchester Grammar School. They sealed what was to become a lifelong friendship by marrying each other's sisters. In 1913 Sieff met and fell under the spell of Chaim Weizmann, then a science lecturer at Manchester University, where Sieff had taken a degree in economics. Sieff became an ardent Zionist and willing unpaid assistant to Weizmann, accompanying him to the postwar peace conferences at Versailles and San Remo and, during the 1920s, acting as his 'eyes and ears' on numerous trips to Palestine. This political involvement ran parallel with his enthusiastic commitment to a business career with Marks and Spencer. In 1915 Simon Marks had invited him onto the board to help him fight off a take-over bid. In 1926 Sieff became joint managing-director and vice-chairman, a position he held until assuming the chairmanship in 1964 on Marks's death. They were essentially complementary, Marks being a desk man and Sieff bustling round the country seeking and sustaining suppliers. On one occasion in the 1930s Sieff invited Oswald Mosley, leader of the nascent British Union of Fascists, to his St John's Wood apartment to discuss the possibility of having him address a group of Jewish businessmen. In the course of their conversation Mosley explained that a struggling political movement had to have a hate object to mobilize and motivate its supporters and for the Fascists this happened to be Jews. The project went no further. Sieff was also a Fellow of the Royal Anthropological Society, a Fellow of the Royal Geographical Society, a connoisseur of claret and the classics and an expert on the breeding of cattle and the growing of strawberries and orchids.

A Shadier Side of the Wood

St John's Wood's reputation for tolerance – or at least discretion – in relation to sexual irregularities, have made it, and adjacent Maida Vale, an attractive area of residence for homosexuals as well as mistresses and brothel-keepers. Virginia Woolf, who was renowned for her extensive and discriminating knowledge of London's topography, referred on occasion with brusque fondness to the 'Bugger Boys of Blomfield Road'.

Edward Fitzgerald (1809-1883), however, would have placed very little strain on any district's tolerance. He took almost as much trouble to avoid fame as most other writers have to seek it. Most of his life he passed in his native Suffolk, contentedly reading, gardening and boating. Solitary, rather than reclusive, by nature, he was regarded as the best of company by those, like Thackeray, with whom he cared to socialise. Independently wealthy, he lived frugally by choice. Scholarly necessity impelled him to London periodically, as in 1843, when he took a house at 24 Greenberry Street.

Few English literary works truly merit the accolade 'unique'. Fitzgerald's version of *The Rubaiyat of Omar Khayyam* is one of the few. Far too free to be called a translation of the original Persian verses composed eight centuries before, it is a masterpiece in its own right, the product of a profound scholarship tempered by exquisite taste. Significantly, its evocations of erotic passion leave the gender of the beloved unspecified.

Ftizgerald's personal life was candidly summarised by the critic Rupert Croft-Cooke: "No man's life makes the mumbo-jumbo of psychologists and Freudians more trivial and absurd. Fitzgerald loved men, particularly two men, and knew no sexual attraction to women. Whether or not he could be called homosexual in medico-legal parlance, whether or not anything he did could have laid him open ... to a charge of gross indecency, is of little consequence. He loved Posh, his big Viking-like fisherman ... Who cares whether or not they went to bed together ?".

The varied life of **Edith Lees Ellis** (1861-1916), novelist, feminist and pioneer socialist, included a nervous breakdown and spells as a teacher and Ramsay MacDonald's secretary before she met and married the pioneer sexologist Havelock Ellis in 1891. After a honeymoon in Paris they agreed that, while they would winter together in Corn-

152. Edward Fitzgerald. Pencil drawing by Spedding.

wall, they would spend their summers apart. Shortly afterwards Edith fell in love with a woman named Claire. Ellis took this development with an equanimity which she failed to reciprocate equally when he confessed being attracted to other women. For Edith, Claire was followed by several others until 1900, when she fell in love with Lily, a painter who lived in the artists' colony at St Ives. In 1902 Lily died at the age of 36. Edith kept a picture of her at her bedside for the rest of her life and communicated with her through a medium. Notwithstanding this ectoplasmic liaison Edith and her husband grew closer as he nursed her devotedly through numerous illnesses. Two lecture tours of the USA revealed a real talent for public speaking and won her headlines in Chicago when she spoke openly in favour of lesbian relationships. But upon her return from the second tour she fell victim to persecution mania and attempted suicide in hospital. The last year of her life, when she was living apart from Ellis at Sandringham Court, Maida Vale, witnessed a partial recovery of her faculties as she formulated

ambitious plan
of plays based
raid on 3rd Sep
watch and pass
complained of t
chill ten days l
John Maundy
in what is now t
when it had beer
1920s, was the '
'fix' a title for an
imprisoned in 192
Park Terrace, sha
although he was
mysteriously in 1
arranged for her t
– indeed below th
Marlow. When her
1933 whatever trac
in her body had al
Yorkshire-born N
and disastrously, tri
as a canteen supervi
factory, she fell in lo
She called herself 'M
acted in small parts
of illness convinced he
in writing. From 1926
books a year. In 1930
live at 29 Alma Squa
bought a villa on Lake
Sadie, would visit her
of the year with her
England. Simmy and th
Hall also visited 'Casa M
puffed on her pipe, dr
regaled them with coar
Between 1941 and 194 ... . the
London stage and worked for ENSA. After the war
she returned to Italy but would broadcast on
Woman's Hour during her annual visits to England.

Hannah Gluckstein (1895-1978), who adopted
the artistic name Gluck, lived with her family at
73 Avenue Road from 1906 until she ran away
during the latter stages of the Great War "with 2s
6d in my pocket and no food card". Her father
was one of the founders of the J. Lyons chain of
tea-shops, and her mother was an opera singer,
from whom Hannah inherited a fine voice. Following St Paul's Girls School, Hannah attended
the St John's Wood School of Art even though her
real ambition at that stage was to follow her mother
in an operatic career. What revolutionised her life
was a portrait of the violin maestro Joachim (*see*
p.92) by John Singer Sargent. The sight of a mere
photograph of the picture, hung up in the artists'

n of the Wigmore Hall, where she was waiting
ike her concert debut was enough: "there was
at whirl of paint ... this hit me plumb in my
plexus, all thoughts of being a singer van-
."

nnah's family allowed her to spend a month
ing in Cornwall and her early efforts received
wing nods from Laura Knight. The prospect
ventional domesticity now appalled her and
npetuously ran away from Avenue Road
he assurance of Alfred Munnings, no less,
would help her if she wished to persevere
er art. Gordon Selfridge also assisted her
iding space in his Oxford Street emporium
she sketched 'instant portraits'. Seeing her
ination, her family provided financial
for her ambitions. She nevertheless made
lic rejection of bourgeois mores by adopt-
ame Gluck, rejecting either first name or
x 'Miss', cropping her hair and dressing
clothes. Her versatility was exhibited in
seascapes, genre pictures, still life and
scenes, presented in a distinctive, three-
ped frame which she patented in 1932.
n avid collector of seashells, fine china
walking-sticks, all of which she used to
effect in her home at Bolton House,
Hill, Hampstead. In her later years she
mewhat obsessive crusade against the
stry regarding the changing quality of
erials, which she believed would im-
urability of their paintings.
rley (1896-1967), who lived in a flat on
in the 1930s, was a lifelong friend of
His triumphantly successful 1925
oners of War drew on his own Great
ce as a prisoner. During the thirties
ne worked as a talks producer for the BBC, then
became the literary editor of *The Listener* (1935-
59). His later writings included novels and autobiography which discussed his homosexuality
with disarming candour.

The Maida Vale flat was witness to a series of
casual liaisons, the longest of which lasted some
four years. Eventually Ackerley found lasting
contentment in the companionship of Queenie, an
adored Alsatian bitch.

W.H. Auden (1907-1973) lodged briefly at fellow poet Stephen Spender's home, 29 Randolph
Crescent, in 1933 and with Spender again, at 15
Loudoun Road in 1963 and 1972, after he had
settled in Austria. During the latter year the
University of London honoured him with an
honorary doctorate but his simultaneous return to
Christ Church, Oxford, where he was given a free
cottage, proved an ill-disguised disaster.

The composer **Benjamin Britten** (1913-1976)

maintained his London base with his lifelong partner **Peter Pears** at 45a St John's Wood High Street between 1943 and 1946 and at 59 Marlborough Place between 1958 and 1963. During Britten's first period of residence his opera *Peter Grimes* received its premiere (1945), during the second his operatic version of *A Midsummer Night's Dream* (1960).

James Pope-Hennessy (1916-1974) grew up at 74 Avenue Road, the home of his father, a major-general, and was still living there when his first book, *London Fabric*, was published in 1939, winning him the Hawthornden Prize. His later publications included travel books and biographies. At thirty he concluded that he was "only capable of companionship tempered by stray sexual obsessions" – one of whom was almost certainly responsible for battering him to death in his flat at Ladbroke Grove. No one was ever charged.

Nancy Spain (1917-1964), a Roedean-educated Geordie, excelled at sport and initially worked as a sports journalist while also playing 'dialect' parts on the radio. Her wartime experiences in the WRNS furnished hilarious material for her first book *Thank You Nelson* (1945). Settling at 4 Randolph Gardens, and supporting herself by freelance journalism, in four years she wrote six novels and a biography of her great-aunt, Mrs Beeton, author of the classic *Book of Household Management*. She moved out of Maida Vale c.1950, shortly before meeting the publisher Joan Werner Laurie (Jonnie), a widow with two young sons, who was to become her partner in 'close disharmony'. During the 1950s Nancy Spain became one of the first TV celebrities, appearing on programmes as different as *My Word* and *Jukebox Jury*. In 1954 she was co-founder of *She* magazine, of which Jonnie was the first editor. They were killed together in the same Piper Apache when it crashed near Aintree, where Nancy was to report the Grand National for the *News of the World*.

Artist **John Minton** (1917-1957), a scion of the china-producing family, attended the St John's Wood School of Art (1935-1938), where he met Michael Ayrton, with whom he then shared a studio in Paris. In 1942 they collaborated on designing the costumes and sets for Gielgud's production of *Macbeth*. In 1943 Minton got himself discharged from the Pioneer Corps by threatening to rape his fellow soldiers. He was subsequently to compound this dramatic 'outing' by writing an open letter to *The Listener*, which J.R. Ackerley ensured was published. From 1946 to 1954 Minton

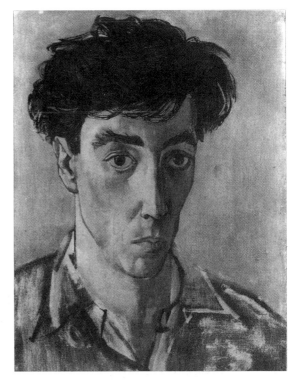

153. John Minton.

lived at 37 Hamilton Terrace with Keith Vaughan, a fellow teacher from Camberwell School of Art, though Minton himself moved on to teach at Central School and then the Royal College of Art. Wherever he taught students benefited both from his creativity and his generosity. Minton's influence was also exerted through the book illustrations, film posters, stage sets and designs for textiles and wallpapers for which he was much in demand. The reassertion of American and French influences on the English art scene in the early 1950s left him behind, unable to respond. Possessing superb graphic skills, he was appalled by the emerging trend of abstraction. After a decade of prodigious productivity Minton's output and influence evaporated rapidly. He plunged into alcoholism, promiscuity and self-absorption. Resigning from the Royal College of Art, Minton went to Spain, produced some fine paintings but returned still dissatisfied and depressed. After an extended drinking bout he took his own life with an overdose.

154. *The area of North Bank, north of the Regent's Canal at the time of railway development in the 1890s. The extension of the Great Central Railway was built to Marylebone Station in this period.*

Envoi

Almost as soon as the building of St John's Wood and Maida Vale was completed their radical reconstruction began. Between 1894 and 1899 the Great Central Railway's extension to its new terminus at Marylebone demolished some twenty streets. During the same decade the building of large-scale apartment blocks began along Maida Vale. Between 1904 and 1905 St John's Wood High Street was almost entirely rebuilt. In the latter year J.G. Head contributed to Volume III of the *London Topographical Record* a survey entitled 'Changing London: Notes on Alterations which have taken place in the northern portion of St Marylebone during the last fifteen years'. His laconic summary of the process of transformation is a minor masterpiece of compression: "The opposition being broken down by the Railway Company, the other invading bodies met with little resistance." The Poplars in Aberdeen Place was demolished to make way for St Marylebone Borough Council's

new Electric Lighting Works. Portland Town– "composed chiefly of small houses, closely packed together, and occupied by a poor class of tenant" – was given a thorough drubbing by the Howard de Walden estate, its new landlord. On the whole Head clearly approved of the changes: "handsome blocks of flats are being erected, flanked by commodious and imposing private residences, while the small houses at the southern end of the Avenue Road are disappearing before the delightfully artistic buildings which are associated with the name of William Willett." Perhaps it was a sense that a visible past was visibly disappearing that prompted Head's own survey and the publication in 1913 of Alan Montgomery Eyre's *Saint John's Wood : Its History, Its Houses, Its Haunts and Its Celebrities*, the most substantial account of the district to appear to that date.

The process of transformation continued in the inter-war period. In 1928 the Eyre Arms was demolished to make way for the construction of the Eyre Court apartment block. In 1935 the artist Frank R. Beresford, who had been a student at the St John's Wood Art School in 1900, complained

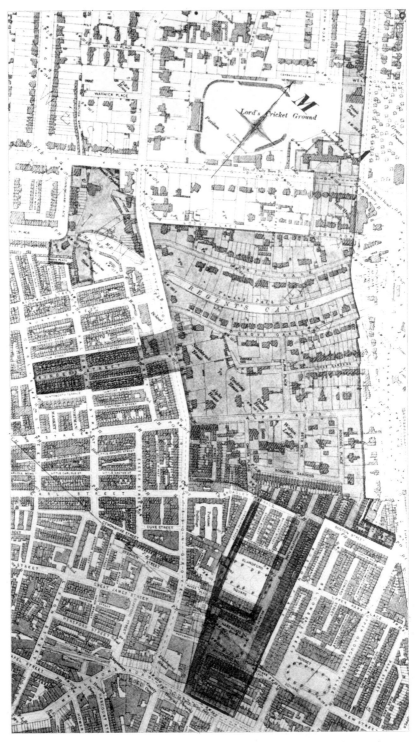

155. The areas of Lisson Grove and the most southern part of St John's Wood
taken by the Great Central Railway, are shaded.

156. *One of the houses in North Bank demolished to make way for the railway.*

157. *St John's Wood High Street at the end of the last century, before the building of mansion flats.*

158. *Mansion flats in St John's Wood High Street c.1906.*

159. *Mansion flats in Elgin Avenue.*

160 and 161. *Townshend Cottages in Portland Town were a target for slum clearance even before the last war. The picture above is from a newspaper cutting of 1936 when tenants were protesting against plans to demolish their homes. Presumably the war intervened and stopped demolition, because the lower picture, taken in 1949, shows the cottages before their removal.*

162 and 163. Two former Underground stations, both closed when the present St John's Wood station was opened in 1939. Above is St John's Wood station opposite Lord's, opened in 1868 as part of the Metropolitan line. Its name was changed to Lord's only six months before it was closed. Below is Marlborough Road station, on the corner of Finchley Road and Queen's Grove. The building still remains, disguised as a Chinese restaurant (see Ill. 164).

164. *The old Marlborough Road station in 1998, now a Chinese restaurant. It is on the corner of Finchley Road and Queen's Grove.*

in an article in *The Evening News* that "no suburb had so marked a personality as the old St. John's Wood ... 'Art Quarter' was written all over it, from the colour shops in the High Street and the groups of students from the School of Art strolling about in their overalls and painting coats to the numerous studios ... the distinctive character of the population has quite disappeared."

In Abbey Road MacWhirter's studio had become a restaurant and H.J. Draper's house had become a garage. Beresford himself clung on, defiantly maintaining a Bohemian lifestyle which epitomised an imagined semi-rural heritage – hens in the garden and home-made elderberry wine. It was a posture with all the permanence of a gesture. In 1937 one hundred and twenty Victorian houses were demolished, on a fifteen acre site bounded by Abbey Road, Loudoun Road, Springfield Road and Boundary Road, to make way for a £420,000 project to build 84 'Georgian' detached villas. (£4,500 for a house with six bedrooms and three bathrooms.)

There were changes too in the provision of Underground railway services. When the Metropolitan line had been extended as long ago as 1868 to Swiss Cottage, two stations were opened in St John's Wood, one called St John's Wood Road, the other Marlborough Road. The former (later renamed Lords) was on the site of the Holiday Inn hotel, and the latter building still remains, now disguised as a Chinese restaurant on the east side of Finchley Road opposite Marlborough Road. Both of these stations were closed when the Bakerloo line was opened in November 1939 and (for some) the more convenient station of St John's Wood was built. The war then brought random destruction with an impartial hand. St Mark's, Hamilton Terrace and the Liberal Synagogue in St John's Wood Road were both substantially damaged.

NEW PROPERTIES

The GEORGIAN TRADITION
at ACACIA GARDENS,
ST. JOHN'S WOOD

Acacia Gardens is a small, dignified residential development in a private road.

Adjacent to St. John's Wood Station.

Only a few minutes from London's West End.

Graceful neo-Georgian three-storey elevations.

An internal plan that makes modern living a pleasure.

These houses are decidedly for the discerning.

ACCOMMODATION: 4 bedrooms, 2 bathrooms, drawing room with balcony, dining room opening on to patio, up-to-date kitchen.

Built with the best of modern materials to an exciting design by leading Architects T. P. Bennett & Son.

Full Central Heating Landscaped Gardens by Richard Sudell, F.I.L.A.

View House decorated by HOUSE & GARDEN *and furnished by* HEALS *of Tottenham Court Road.*
Open weekdays to 8 p.m. and Sundays to 6 p.m.

99-YEAR LEASE
£9,750
to
£9,950
including garage.
Ground Rent £55 per annum.

WATES BUILT HOMES LTD.

165. *New 'Georgian' houses in Acacia Road in 1959, with 99-year leases at under £10,000*

The disappearance of familiar landmarks was offset by the establishment of new institutions – Abbey Road recording studios in 1931, the King's Troop, Royal Horse Artillery in 1946. In 1952 St John's Wood Church was at last designated as a parish church. A St John's Wood Preservation Society was established in 1956. An adventure playground came into being in 1957 and Quintin Kynaston School in 1958. In 1963 the St John's Wood Society was re-established and in 1965 St Marylebone almshouses were rebuilt. The rebuilding of the Barracks was completed in 1972.

If Landseer and Spencer, Bradlaugh and Blondin, George Eliot and Thomas Lord were ghosts but dimly remembered, they had been replaced by characters no less distinctive. Little Venice was the haunt of John Julius Norwich and Lady Diana Cooper, Elizabeth Jane Howard, Joan Collins and Arthur Lowe. The inimitable commentator Brian Johnstone had become the presiding deity of Lord's. St John's Wood and Maida Vale continued to be, as Eyre had once summarised it with elegant simplicity, "*par excellence* the district for interesting people".

166 and 167. Two images of St John's Wood long past. Above is a hand laundry in Queen's Grove next to the old Underground station. The Blanchisserie boasted of Kate, 'our mainstay who has been washing linen entirely by hand for over 50 years'. The laundry had closed by 1957. Below is Mr and Mrs Parker's restaurant in Addison House, Grove End Road, mainly intended for professional women.

Chronology

1086 Manor of Lilestone surveyed in Domesday Book

1323 St John's Wood assigned to the Hospital of the Knights of St John of Jerusalem

1538 Marylebone Park established for royal hunting

1553 St John's Wood restored to the Knights of St John

1559 St John's Wood reclaimed by the Crown

1574 John Lyon bequeathes land for the upkeep of the Harrow Road

1586 Conspirator Anthony Babington hides in St John's Wood

1650 St John's Wood sold to William Clarke of Inner Temple

1668 St John's Wood granted by Charles II to Lord Arlington in settlement of debts

1732 Henry Samuel Eyre purchases 45 fields from the 4th Earl of Chesterfield

1793 Pine Apple Nursery established

1794 Eyre Estate surveyed

1801 Population of St Marylebone parish 63,982

1804 Artillerymen stationed at St. John's Wood Farm

1811 Development of Regent's Park begins

1811-1820 Regent's Canal built

1812 Clergy Orphan School established on the future Wellington Road

1814 Lord's Cricket Ground opens on its present site
St John's Wood Chapel consecrated

1820 Eyre Arms Tavern and Assembly Rooms designed by John White Jr.

1823 Col. Henry Samuel Eyre inherits the Eyre Estate
Cavalry Riding Establishment moved from Pimlico to St John's Wood

1824 Edwin Landseer settles in St. John's Wood

1825 New Army riding school building completed

1826 Wellington Road opened

1827 Act of Parliament authorises the construction of New Finchley Road

1831 Population of St Marylebone parish 122,206

1836 St. Marylebone parish almshouses built
Roman Catholic church, Grove Road consecrated

1838 School for the Blind established in Upper Avenue Road

1839 Eglinton Tournament rehearsals held at Eyre Arms

1841 Queen's Grove and Queen's Terrace named to mark the wedding of Victoria and Albert
Swiss Cottage Tavern opened

1846 Maida Vale Cricket Club founded

1847 St Mark's Hamilton Terrace consecrated

1851 Presbyterian Church, Carlton Hill built
New College of Independent Dissenters opened

1859 St Paul's, Avenue Road opened

1868 St John's Wood Road Station opened

1870 St John's Wood Fire Station opened in Adelaide Road

1871 Swiss Cottage tollgate abolished

1873 Parish schools, Violet Hill rebuilt

1874 Macclesfield Bridge explosion in Regent's Park

1878 St John's Wood School of Art established

1882 New London Synagogue built

1887 Lord's takes over former Henderson's nursery as a practice ground

1892 Sir Isaac Newton public house built
The Crown Hotel (Crocker's Folly) opened

1894-1899 Great Central Railway extension demolishes twenty streets to the south of St John's Wood

1899 St John's Wood Chapel becomes a chapel at ease to Christ Church, Cosway Street

1901 Hospital of St John and St Elizabeth moves to St John's Wood

1902 Hospital for Nervous Diseases moves to St. John's Wood

1904-5 St John's Wood High Street rebuilt

1925 Liberal Synagogue built

1928 Eyre Arms demolished to make way for Eyre Court

1931 Abbey Road recording studios opened

1937 Demolition of 120 Victorian houses

1939 Marlborough Road Station closed
St John's Wood Road (Lord's) Station closed

1946 King's Troop, Royal Horse Artillery established

1952 St John's Wood Church designated as a parish church

1956 St John's Wood Preservation Society established

1957 St John's Wood adventure playground established

1958 Quintin Kynaston School built

1963 St John's Wood Society re-established

1964 St John's Wood Synagogue built

1965 St Marylebone almshouses rebuilt

1969 Beatles' *Abbey Road* album recorded

1972 Rebuilding of St John's Wood Barracks completed

1974 All Saints church closed

Further Reading

E. Bright Ashford: *St John's Wood: The Harrow School and Eyre Estates* (St Marylebone Society Publications No. 8 1965)

Arthur Ashbridge: *St Marylebone and Its Anglo-Saxon Manors* (*Transactions of the London and Middlesex Archaeological Society* 1918. Reprinted by the Author)

Rosemary Ashton: *Little Germany: Exile and Asylum in Victorian England* (OUP 1986)

Richard Bowden: *Britain in Old Photographs: Marylebone and Paddington* (Sutton 1995)

W.S. Clarke: *The Suburban Homes of London: A Residential Guide* (Chatto and Windus 1881)

Ann Cox-Johnson: *Handlist to the Ashbridge Collection on the history and topography of St Marylebone* (Borough of St Marylebone, 1959)

Ann Cox-Johnson: *Handlist of Painters, Sculptors and Architects associated with St Marylebone 1760-1960* (Borough of St Marylebone 1963)

Richard Dorment: *Alfred Gilbert* (Yale University Press 1985)

Alan Montgomery Eyre: *Saint John's Wood: Its History, Its Houses, Its Haunts and Its Celebrities* (Chapman and Hall 1913)

Anthony Feiling: *A History of the Maida Vale Hospital for Nervous Diseases* (Butterworth 1958)

Antony Grant: *A Walk Through the Wood* (1977)

F.H. Hallam: *Random Sketches of the Parish of St Marylebone* (1885)

George Higgins: *A History of St John's Wood* (Institute of Estate and House Estate Agents 1900)

London Topographical Record Vol. III and Vol. XXVII

Gordon Mackenzie: *Marylebone: Great City North of Oxford Street* (Macmillan 1972)

Stella Margetson: *An Abode Of Love and The Arts* (St John's Wood Society 1988)

Aubrey Noakes: *William Frith: Extraordinary Victorian Painter* (Jupiter 1978)

John Oliver and Peter Bradshaw: *St John's Wood Church 1814-1955* (The church, 1955).

E.G. Semple: All Saints' Church, St John's Wood Centenary 1846-1946 (All Saints' Church 1946)

F.H.W. Sheppard: *Local Government in St Marylebone 1688-1835* (Athlone Press 1958).

Cecil Smith: *A Short History of St John's Wood and Some of Its Former Inhabitants* (Wilding 1942)

Thomas Smith: *A Topographical and Historical Account of the Parish of St Marylebone* (1833)

J.C.C. Sworder: 'Centenary at the Wood' (*Royal Artillery Journal* CVII 1980)

Victoria County History of Middlesex Vol IX

E. Walford: *Old and New London* Vol. 5 (Cassell, Petter and Galpin 1894)

Charles White: *St Marylebone: Past and Present* (Ed. J. Burrow & Co. n.d.)

Jack Whitehead: *The Growth of St Marylebone and Paddington* (Jack Whitehead 1989)

W.H. Wilson: *Centenary: St Mark's Church, Hamilton Terrace* (1947)

Some Name Derivations

A number of local street names are decidedly sylvan - such as Acacia and Elm Tree. Others have a Scottish bias, especially in Maida Vale (Elgin, Lauderdale, Lanark) and yet others there are boringly named, and it seems at random, after English place names (Chichester, Chevening, Saltram, Stafford etc.). Others are intended to suggest a high class of development (Clifton, Carlton etc.). But a number of streets have more specific origins.

Abbey Road: Nearby Kilburn Priory was attached to the Abbey of Westminster.

Abercorn Place: Lord Abercorn was a governor of Harrow School, on whose estate the road was built.

Aberdeen Place: Lord Aberdeen was also a governor of Harrow School.

Allitsen Road: after nearby resident, the composer, Mary Allitsen

Alpha Road: the first street built on the Eyre Estate.

Barrow Hill Road: Barrow Hill is next to Primrose Hill. Despite its name, no evidence of a burial site has been found.

Blenheim Road: after Marlborough's victory at Blindheim.

Blomfield Road: Charles Blomfield, Bishop of London.

Boundary Road: boundary between St Marylebone parish and Hampstead parish.

Cavendish Avenue and Close: land owned by Cavendish family

Circus Road: reflects the circular shape of the original Eyre Estate building plan

Fairlop Place and Oak Tree Road: Fairlop Oak. a celebrated tree in Essex.

Greenberry Street: possibly a corruption of Green Barrow Hill.

Hall Road: builder William Hall.

Hamilton Terrace: Charles Hamilton was a Harrow School governor.

Kingsmill Terrace: member of the Eyre family

Langford Place: owner of Lileston manor in 14th century

Lisson Grove: manor of Lileston

Loudoun: most likely from John Loudon, landscape gardener.

Lyons Place: John Lyon founded Harrow School

Mackennal Street: Bertram Mackennal, sculptor, lived nearby

Maida Vale: a battle in the Peninsular War (1806) in Spain.

Marlborough Hill and Place: the Duke of Marlborough

Northwick Terrace: Lord John Northwick, Harrow School governor.

Nugent Terrace: Lord Nugent MP for Aylesbury lived in Langford Place, and Fld Marshal Sir George Nugent lived in St John's Wood during his retirement.

Ordnance Road: The Board of Ordnance, the original lessee of St John's Wood Barracks.

Randolph Avenue: Lord Randolph Churchill, a local MP

St John's Wood: land owned by the Knights of St John

Scott-Ellis Gardens: Built by Thomas Scott-Ellis, 8th Baron Howard de Walden.

Townshend Road: the commander who received the French surrender at Quebec *c*.1759.

Walpole Mews: Walpole Eyre

INDEX

Asterisks denote illustrations and captions.